Nikki!!..
You are such a
boss Queen!!.. Thank
you so much for
having me today!!
You were born to
Slay!!

XO
ly,

Credit: Tasia Wells

ABOUT THE AUTHOR

Rachel McCord is a model (featured in: *Vogue, Glamour, etc.*), star and producer of *The Rachel McCord Show: From Trailer Parks to Red Carpets*, speaker (*UCLA, Share.Like.Buy,* etc.), and philanthropist.

Passionate about leveraging emergent media platforms to help talent like herself accomplish their dreams, she works tirelessly to inspire others that no matter where you come from, you can live a full and fabulous life.

As a serial entrepreneur based in Hollywood, she collaborates with, advises, and encourages her network of fellow talent, celebrities, bloggers, and influencers on all things related to branding, social media, and Hollywood.

She is frequently featured by some of the biggest outlets in the world (*TMZ, Radar, Star, Daily Mail,* etc.) and currently resides in West Hollywood with husband and business partner, Rick Schirmer. Schirmer has produced over 200 marketing campaigns for enterprises like *Friends, Disney, Wal-Mart, The Hangover, Purge, Harry Potter,* and *The Chronicles of Narnia.*

"*Rachel McCord is that elusive combination of being both glamorous and genuine—all in one glamorous package. Beautiful inside and out—she exudes charisma and charm in spades. But above all–Rachel is a consummate professional who brings her A-game to whatever she does.*" – **Heidi Nazarudin, Award-winning blogger (TheAmbitionista.com) and founder of Blogger Babes.**

"*Your work with Jillian has given her so much confidence. Thank you for what you are doing for our daughter.*" – **Marla, Mom and Entrepreneur**

If you want to make it in the new digital age of millennial Hollywood, I would recommend you pick up Rachel McCord's incredible book: SLAY THE FAME GAME." – **Russell Stuart, Hollywood Manager**

"*All the tips and information you gave helped tremendously/ and I appreciate all the help that you have given me thus far. [I] brought my following up, from the small amount of 250 people I had, to over 1,900+ followers and still growing each day ... I am in the works of possibly creating the clothing attire and styling for the gym corporation, Lifetime Fitness.*" – **Tommy, Stylist**

"*I work alongside many celebs as co-founder of Obsev Studios. Seeing how far Rachel McCord had come since she was first a guest on Hollyscoop is amazing! She definitely knows what she is doing when it comes to building a brand. But her heart to serve others is even more impressive!*" – **Diana Madison, Low Down with Diana Madison**

"*[Rachel] is an amazing inspiration. She is the sweetest and most genuine person ever! She has helped me tremendously and I love collaborating with her!*" –**Erin Nicole, Blogger**

"*I'm fabulous because [Rachel] inspires me.*" – **Carol Gontijo, Social Media Influencer**

"*Rachel has taught me to always believe in myself ... never give up!*" – **Star, Pretty Little Liars**

"*I can't tell you enough how much [your help] meant to me. Your message was a godsend. It made me cry. You gave me hope yesterday, and I want you to know you were a ray of sunshine for my family. I loved your ideas about my music. I can't thank you enough. I truly, truly can't thank you enough. Thank you for listening to my song. Thank you for your feedback. I needed to hear some of those things you said today. You are truly an inspiration.*" – **Sheena, Singer**

Credit: Kelly McKeever

SLAY THE FAME GAME

Written by Rachel McCord

Cover photo credit: Britt Barrett
Creative direction for the cover by Michael Bezjian | The Artists Project
Illustration by Alphie Chikwashi

LAUNCHPRENEUR
MEDIA HOUSE

ISBN 978-0-692-90624-8

www.slaythefamegame.com

QUANITY PURCHASES & APPEARANCES:

Special discounts are available on quantity purchases by bookstores, wholesalers, nonprofit organizations, corporations, associations, and others.

For more information or to schedule author appearances, please contact The McCord List at Hello@TheMcCordList.com.

Entertainment; Self Help; Entrepreneur
First Edition

CHAPTERS

P.S. Don't skip my Acknowledgements on page 141!

Credit: Britt Barrett

INTRODUCTION

According to the U.S. Media and Entertainment Spotlight, the entertainment industry is expected to reach **$771 billion** in revenue in 2019... **blah, blah, blah.**

GOT YA!!! Let's be honest. You didn't pick up this book to learn this is the most competitive industry in the world. Duh. We know. Or that less than 0.01% of people actually make it. No surprise there.

We know the majority of the millions who load up their cars and move to Hollywood or sign up as social media stars will fail. We saw them on I-10 East, heading home with holes in their hearts and wallets.

It doesn't take a rocket scientist (which is great because I'm not one) to know you need a solid plan, sexy brand, and killer networking skills to make it. <insert me here>

I'm going to teach you how to:

- Monetize
- Slay your style
- Build a platform
- Stay sane

- Grow your social media following
- Collaborate and network effectively
- Deal with haters and cyberbullies (eww)
- Literally SLAY THE FAME GAME

Look, I am <u>not</u> the most famous person in the world.
In fact, I'm a couple letters down on the "List" ...

But, I've got eight years experience in the entertainment industry, with over 1.5 billion+ in press impressions (since last year) with *Cosmopolitan, Glamour, Vogue, Daily Mail, Forbes...*

Credit: Britt Barrett

All of which I've leveraged to get my own talk show, network of fellow influencers and celebs, speaking engagements, and well, this book you're reading right now!

My insane career in Hollywood has taught me so much. That's why, as fellow talent, I figured the book section deserved a sexy little facelift. And you, Queen, deserved my eight years of dos and don'ts to help you build (or upgrade) your own brand.

If you want to play lottery with your career, put this book down and be my guest. However, if you're ready to pull back the curtain and learn how magazine covers, red carpets, tons of press, parties, and success can also become your life ... grab a mocktail and keep reading!

Credit: Kelly McKeever

P.S. Don't worry. This book isn't boring. I can't stand that crap. And, it's not full of hypothetical situations I thought up over champagne and a manicure.

Who wants to have to guess if an author actually knows any of the crap they're talking about? Not you. You don't want to waste time or money on another stupid dust catcher of a book. That's as boring as a bad commercial and helpful as an expired coupon.

I'm not gonna waste your time. I'm legit. In fact, I believe in this book's ability to help you with everything from non-lame therapy to Instagram verification, I'll send you a copy for free. Just say hello@themccordlist.com.

This book isn't just about walking red carpets and looking fab (although, duh, we'll cover that); it's about loving yourself, believing you can make it, and laughing your way through the mistakes, rejections, and disappointments that come.

NOW LET'S GET INTO IT...
(before this gets weird)

Ricky,
This is for you.
Thank you for
believing in me when I
couldn't. Credit for this
LAUNCH goes to you
and God.

CHAPTER 1

FROM TRAILER PARKS TO RED CARPETS:
Who the (Bleep) is Rachel McCord?!

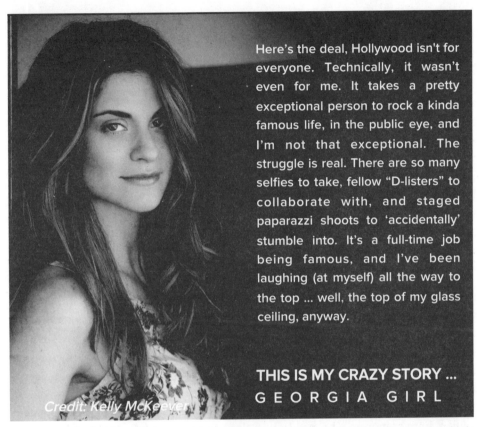

Here's the deal, Hollywood isn't for everyone. Technically, it wasn't even for me. It takes a pretty exceptional person to rock a kinda famous life, in the public eye, and I'm not that exceptional. The struggle is real. There are so many selfies to take, fellow "D-listers" to collaborate with, and staged paparazzi shoots to 'accidentally' stumble into. It's a full-time job being famous, and I've been laughing (at myself) all the way to the top ... well, the top of my glass ceiling, anyway.

THIS IS MY CRAZY STORY ...
G E O R G I A   G I R L

Credit: Kelly McKeever

Oh, hi, new human friend! I don't know why I just said that, but whatever. I think it's probably because I'm a total dork nerd. I figured we should go ahead and get that awkward confession out of the way so you could get to know me. I love long walks on the beach, sassy ladies, and tall glasses of champs when I'm feeling classy (*cheer*) ... What? You wanted to get to know me, right?

Growing up, we didn't have a lot. I was always that kid who ate off-brand cereal, prayed our utilities wouldn't get shut off, and lived in pretty little trailer parks. Okay, they weren't very pretty, and I definitely didn't *love* them ... but a girl has to have an imagination and some rose-colored glasses ... don't you think?

9

You can't choose how you grow up, but you can choose where you go after. If you think I'm going to use this moment to share sob stories with a side order of ice cream and *"hug me, please,"* you're wrong. Sure, I went through some crappy drama growing up. I've dealt with some abuse and lame crap like that, but instead of it making me a weak little hermit, I became a sassy Queen with a fire that drives me every day.

That's right, I just called myself a "Queen," while my childhood would clearly say otherwise. And, no, I'm not talking about Queen of the Trailer Park (although I defs think I would at least place in that competition). It's because I think we're all Queens. So, from now on, that's who you are in my book (literally). If there's one thing I've learned from years of feeling otherwise, it is that we're all powerful Queens who are stronger than we know! So, take a deep breath and go ahead and start loving the diamond that you are. This is coming from someone who has had to fight to love herself and *finally* does ... most of the time.

I don't believe where you come from limits you. Do you? I hope not! I don't think "it" can make you into anything. That's what passion, hard work, and your brain are for. I think how you respond to life shows your true colors. Look, I realize I sound like a cheeseball. I'm very sensitive at my core, so it pops out every now and then, but I'm definitely not weak. I've been bullied, crushed, and put down. But I wasn't going down without a fight ... and neither should you!

When I first moved to Hollywood in 2009, I somehow underestimated the whole 'move cross-country' thing. I remember thinking, "*Ahhh, I can always move home.*" Um, hi, it's a really big deal to pick up your entire life and move to Hollywood. No one prepared me for the commitment to insane traffic, flighty relationships, and the overpriced rent it would take to be "someone" out here. I was homeschooled in Georgia, before it was the trendy "*I travel a lot*" thing to do. So, putting myself out there was really uncomfortable at first.

I made the decision to move during awards season when I came to visit my sisters, Angel and AnnaLynne McCord, in Hollywood. I bounced from red carpet to red carpet, gifting suite to celeb hotspot after becoming friends with the publicists, event planners, and game changers who manage the clipboard at the door. More on that later ... I was kinda in. I mean, how could I say no to that and the opportunity to live with my sisters again? I knew it was going to take some adjusting, but I underestimated just how much. I basically thought, you only live once and I'm young. And, as one of my favorite role models, Kathy Dinsmore, once said, home will always be there. So, to hell with it! Why not? I had always been a 'play it safe, live by the rules' kinda girl ... my childhood was STRICT, y'all! But it was time I broke a few rules and lived a little.

Credit: Alphie Chikwashi

RED CARPET CULTURE SHOCK

Most people come out here all alone to hustle and get their break. But, my Hollywood life, from day one, has been *very* different. I moved out of Georgia and immediately onto red carpets with my sisters. The great news for me (and now you) is I've been learning about legit Hollywood—from a talent and business perspective—from day one. The bad news is, when you have no guidance and are getting tons of attention, you can make some really big mistakes in front of some really big people ... very fast.

Credit: Britt Barrett

The shift in my life was culture shock x crazy for a million reasons. One of the biggest ones happened two weeks after I arrived. I was walking through a Ralph's checkout (the weird name of our grocery stores out here), when I was dumbfounded to see a picture of my sister and I on the cover of the Enquirer Magazine with the title, "*Who's gay in Hollywood?*" Ummm, WHAT!? Well, first of all, I can solve your little cliff hanger right now ... NOT US!! Eww! Secondly, that's disgusting, she's my SISTER, please go away. Thank you very ~~much~~ gross. I love my sister and all, but ... umm, really ...? Little by little, I was learning about the fame game. Of course, at the moment, in the checkout line, I had no idea what I was doing with my brand. I didn't even know I had one so I definitely wasn't putting any energy behind a strategy. I just did what any sane person would do in this situation. I bought the entire stack of magazines so no one else could! I was protecting a brand I didn't even know I would create one day.

I think the first time I realized I was living a pretty dope life was when I showed up at an award show. I can't really remember which one ... Maybe it was the Globes or something, and I bumped into Morgan Freeman. I was like, "*Umm, you are Morgan Freeman.*" His response: "*Yes, I am.*" We obviously had a moment. I crack myself up ... kinda. Anyway, I left one massive star moment to run into another: Jessica Simpson. That was the first time we met. P.S. I am one of those nerds who obsesses over her collections, so I didn't hate that moment. She wasn't the sweetest, but I still rock her bright purple pumps with pride. That night I was rolling deep with a ton of celebs. From Anne Hathaway to Michelle Rodriquez and everyone in between. I was literally feelin' myself. JUST KIDDING! I actually wasn't. All I kept thinking was, "*Umm, who let me in?*" Hollywood has a way of making you feel inadequate. Especially if you accidentally compare yourself to anyone else. Plus, confidence isn't one of those things I was gifted with. It was a learned trait. I would just show it on the outside. Everyone knows confidence is attractive, and I wanted to be attractive, so I let that faux confidence RIP. Not rest in peace, "rip" ... duh.

PROFESSIONAL PLUS ONE

With family in the industry, but no clue who I was, I quickly became a professional plus one. Oh, did you not know that's a thing? That's because it's not. It's a concept someone tossed at me in a crappy hater comment. Thanks, nameless troll. The truth is, he was kinda right. By the way, I'm not sure it was a dude, it could have been a girl with a little too much haterade at dinner. Who knows! Either way, they weren't feeling the Rachel McCord vibes. But, that's okay. I wasn't really feeling them either.

If you check out any of my old red carpet images from 2009 on, when I first moved out here, you can tell I wasn't feelin' myself. What I was feeling was insecure, out of my league, and like a professional loser. I don't know what it is about Hollywood or social media, but you can quickly feel like the biggest loser who doesn't measure up and is diagnosed with full-time FOMO for all the parties you weren't invited to. Hi, Met Gala. Can we be properly introduced, please?

I've always been that girl who liked being behind the scenes. Probably because of how much I was put down as a kid. I didn't really want to be noticed. Being invisible felt much better. The problem with Hollywood is that there are two gears: famous or nobody. I was in that weird crack of Hollywood where I wasn't really famous, but I also wasn't a nobody. I was celeb adjacent. Which is basically the crack of Hollywood, unless you know how to leverage it. Which, I'm going to share tips on later ...

WHEN IN DOUBT, DRESS UP FOR GROCERIES

We went through that weird phase where paps would stalk our house on the daily. I would get papped (photographed by paparazzi) at the grocery store, and people would comment on my shots saying how "thrown together" I looked (yeah! I was at the freaking grocery store!! I didn't know the Fashion Police would be judging) and what a "witchy nose" I had. I'm pretty sure that's not a good thing. Note to self: Don't read the comments.

Don't worry, the hater troll section is coming. Oh, and by the way, I'm excited to share everything I've learned so far! From helping my sister to hosting shoots with talent, working with brands, teaching branding tips, and surviving being *kinda* famous myself (emphasis on *kinda*) ... It makes me happy that all my random experiences finally have purpose. That I might be able to help you SLAY the game even more! If I can help one person succeed, love themselves a little more, or break into entertainment without it breaking them ... it makes every fail, tear, hour of work, and question of "WTF" worth it.

Credit: Britt Barrett

BUILDING A BRAND

I wish I had developed my brand before I moved to Hollywood. We wouldn't have had to start from scratch when I met my hubby—aka my launch GENIUS, Rick Schirmer—years after I moved here. But I never would have understood all the insecurities that come up, or even done it without him. So it was all meant to be! Not only did he help me FINALLY believe in myself, he told me I was using my sparkly Sergio Rossi stilettos to run from my potential ... and he was right. I had avoided lots of cameras when I first got out here because I was scared and didn't want to be "known for nothing." Of course, now I'm writing a book on fame ... But, let's just skip right

Rick started helping me brand myself, which was SUCH a dream because he was involved in brand strategy at Disney! Oh, and nineteen years of film and TV marketing didn't hurt either. The man has literally done everything from The Purge to The Hobbit, Blair Witch Project, The Hangover, Tangled, etc. I know I can't count his MBA and studies from Oxford and Pepperdine as my achievements, but he has taught me tons of stuff that I'm passing on to you. But, before you close this book and buy his at RickSchirmer.com (and you should read it, by the way), you should know, I'm a guest speaker for the Film and TV Marketing program at UCLA. **BOOM** (that was the sound of my MIC drop).

After working on my brand, we decided to focus on building a career on the business side of the industry. I was in that stage where I wanted to find my passion and make sense of all these "random" choices and opportunities in my life. My brand looked like a bunch of events, photoshoots, and meetings, but I knew I was more than that. But what? How do you pull all that together and create a brand that works? And, as you do, how do you monetize? No, really, how do you do that? I'm just kidding. I'm obviously going to teach you that in this book ...

DON'T WORRY, WE'RE ALMOST DONE WITH STORY TIME! LMAO.

Finding Purpose

As I was figuring things out, I started booking on-camera segments and modeling gigs with brands like **PUMA, Macy's, MAC Cosmetics,** etc. So, I decided to lean into that more and see what could come of it. Modeling is fun because you get to be girly, play dress up, and work with some of those most talented creative directors and photographers in the business.

Credit: Alphie Chikwashi

Still, I had come from a humble childhood, so I needed a brand with a deeper purpose.

I had literally traded trailer parks for red carpets (lemme, lemme upgrade ya!), but I was still holding myself back. But why? I had healed from trauma-based depression, so I needed to find a way to help others by loving them where they were in life. With sassy love, of course. *Hair flip*

That's when it hit me. I was uniquely qualified to help people in the entertainment industry! It's one of the most nerve-wracking, lonely, and empty industries in the world. All the rejection, drama, insecurities, and crap we deal with EVERY DAY just to book one gig is crazy. But, in order to inspire anyone else, I needed to work twice as hard to overcome the natural desire I have to hide out, blend in, and live simply. I knew I needed to make something of my life. I wanted to inspire that Queen living in a trailer park or crappy one bedroom, Hollywood apartment right now that she could do it too! That she is stronger than she realizes! That I believe in her (aka YOU). We're going to be BFFs and I'm going to encourage you every step of the way. Invite me to a red carpet and I will think of 13 reasons why I can't go. But invite me into your heart where I can help you believe in yourself, love your life, and live your dream? Done!

Sure, that all sounded great, but it was also scary AF. How would people around me react? I was always the bubbly one in a party dress. Was I going to show my true colors and my corny heart? Of course I was! I pulled out some of those thousand self-help books I had read, and started making notes. It was time I share what I had learned from Dr. Wayne Dyer, Louise Hay, Jeff Olson, Joyce Meyer, Stephen Covey, and every one in between. I had the tools and knowledge, I just needed to give myself permission to step into my purpose and be the encouragement Queen I was meant to be!

With that strategy and TONS of work, everything happened so fast! In two years, I had gone from Hollywood irrelevance (fame fades quick) to being invited to tons of events and collaborating with some of the best in the industry. Over champagne and selfies, I started sharing advice, hosting workshops, and being the goodbye call when my celeb friends were done with the industry and wanted out. I would (and literally have) run to their houses (when the two minute Uber wait was too long) to hold them and remind them of the beautiful purpose they have in

Credit: Britt Barrett

their lives. That they can't give up. It may seem like celebs have it all, but when you see the ups in the industry long enough, you start to see the downs.

Today, I'm living a dream I didn't even know I had.

My favorite moments are on my couch, with my friends in the industry, when we get to honestly talk about the crap in this business until we're laughing at the things that sucked five minutes prior. Oh, and don't think I'm just talking about people getting their start. I'm talking about full on, massively successful celebs who struggle with the same insecurities you have. The smartest thing I sniffed out my first month in Hollywood was that to "them" (photographers and industry people), you're only worth as much as someone will pay for your last picture. That is why to *you,* you need to be worth the world.

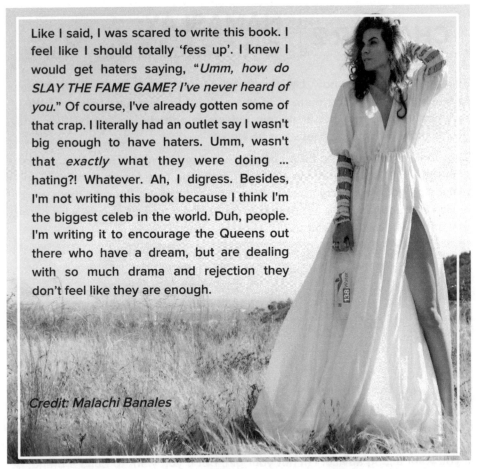

Like I said, I was scared to write this book. I feel like I should totally 'fess up'. I knew I would get haters saying, *"Umm, how do SLAY THE FAME GAME? I've never heard of you."* Of course, I've already gotten some of that crap. I literally had an outlet say I wasn't big enough to have haters. Umm, wasn't that *exactly* what they were doing ... hating?! Whatever. Ah, I digress. Besides, I'm not writing this book because I think I'm the biggest celeb in the world. Duh, people. I'm writing it to encourage the Queens out there who have a dream, but are dealing with so much drama and rejection they don't feel like they are enough.

Credit: Malachi Banales

I work in an industry I couldn't even imagine as a kid, let alone one I expected to succeed in. Of course I've felt inadequate. I still ask myself if I'll ever be enough. Just little ol' me. No makeup, no cameras, no red carpets. Turns out a lot of my friends feel that way too. Which means *you* might. Whether you're renting a room or a bed in an apartment barely making ends meet as you go for the dream, or are on 100% bankroll from your parents, you deserve to know that you're fabulous and I believe in you.

People in this industry will try to chew you up, spit you out, laugh at you, then all of a sudden want every photo they can snag when you make it. But you're smarter, stronger, and more prepared than the hundreds of people creating their social media profiles and moving to Hollywood right now. You've got me. It's a long road from trailer parks to red carpets, but if my sisters and I can do it, you too can achieve anything, no matter where you come from.

CHAPTER 2

NAMASLAY:
Get Started & Stay Sane

Enough about me (for now, LMAO). It's your turn to go for it. And, who better to teach you everything there is to know about this industry than me? Well, technically, there are better people but we're already in Chapter two, and you're stuck with me ... so let's just go with it.

This book is not meant to be a huge bore, full of Hollywood crap that anyone could say, like: how to get into character, arrive on time for every casting, and make sure you slay every dance class created. Although I'm sure that's great advice ... it sounds like a lot of fluff to me. I know tons of people who do all that and never become famous.

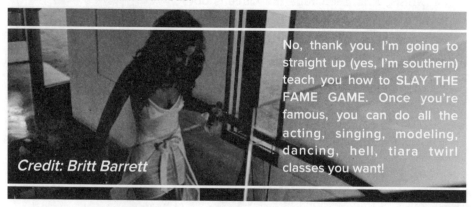

Credit: Britt Barrett

No, thank you. I'm going to straight up (yes, I'm southern) teach you how to SLAY THE FAME GAME. Once you're famous, you can do all the acting, singing, modeling, dancing, hell, tiara twirl classes you want!

If you want acting advice, I'm not your girl. But if you want to build a brand, be famous, and not get burned out, packed up, and ready to pull the plug, I'm your girl. This industry is effin' hard. Don't walk into it without a good sense of self confidence. I'm not talking about a narcissistic, prideful, "*I am perfect*" vibe. Eww, no. I've dated enough of those anyway. Nah, I'm talking about hardcore, legit confidence. The kind that says, it's okay to love and accept yourself. You've got this. Don't give up.

Since this business runs on relationships, it is easy to forget that not all of these people are your friends. Many people will be kissing that gorgeous derriere in hopes of getting something from you. And, no matter how fun the party, you're still working. This is still a job. It's hard on the heart. That's why, if you aren't Beyoncé level confident in who you are and what you do, you'll be struggling ASAP. Don't waste years of high rent and always the callback (never the leading lady), before you check yourself and protect that fragile (and beautiful) heart of yours.

SLAY THAT SELF CARE

Credit: Malachi Banales

I really wish someone had taught me this when I started my career in the industry. I mean, there's a reason I wouldn't rewatch any of my work on TV or film. I felt like a total nerd and judged myself all the way down to my teeth (literally). Focus on your wins not your flaws. You are FABULOUS. You have to start creating healthy habits right now to protect your heart in this industry.

Don't be a wild Queen who goes out every night then sleeps 'til noon ... and is still drunk. No one likes that person. Most importantly, you won't like her. Trust me. Be the person who maintains a fab lifestyle but stays healthy and down to earth in the process. I might love my Captain Crunch, but I know when my body needs a carrot or a nap.

Your schedule in this industry is inconsistent AF. The pressure is intense so you need to take care of yourself and keep your energy camera-ready at all times. I'm not talking about hair and makeup ... yet. We will get to that later. I'm talking health/energy wise. Create a routine that keeps you sane and ready for success. If not, you might feel like your life lacks purpose and start slipping into unhealthy habits with unhealthy people.

I start every day with a suuuper healthy smoothie, devotionals, and a long walk with my puppies. Although I do a pretty good job of relaxing while I work, that is pretty much the end of my chill time because after that I hop right into a stressful scan of my to do list, followed by about eight to ten (or seventeen) hours of work. Surprisingly, I rarely feel drained from hard work. When I focus on positive thoughts, it takes a lot to get me down. Oh, and I always do the crap I don't like FIRST ... I feel like a BOSS after!

SMOOTHIE RECIPE

2 cups of coconut water
2 cups of kale and spinach blend
3 cups of frozen fruit medley
1 tablespoon of flax seeds
1 tablespoon of honey
Blend well ...
VOILA!

Tony Hsieh, CEO of Zappos, has some pretty epic advice on managing emails (one of my least favorite things EVER). He recommends spending your morning, until noon, replying to all emails from the day before. He never replies to an email on the same day it arrives. That way, he is always only one day behind, and emails don't control his entire day (or life)!

Credit: Kelly McKeever

COMMIT TO GROWTH

I'm sure you're thinking:

"Great life advice, but can I just be FAMOUS already?"

Well, at least that's what I assume you're thinking (it's really hard to write a book because all of a sudden it's like you're supposed to read minds and know what everyone else is thinking). Whatever.

We all wish we could just skip to the part where we become famous, but I'm not Mrs. Claus and, unless your daddy owns NBC (in which case, *can we be friends?*), it is going to be a long process. But, don't worry, every crazy, long journey begins with one step. Or whatever those super serious, self-help gurus say. The point is, settle in, it's gonna be a long ride. My sister hit fame three years after moving to Hollywood, but that was insanely fast ... and it was still eight years after she started out.

Most people never change until the annoyance of where they are becomes more annoying than the process of change itself. So get annoyed. Life is all about growth and I'm obsessed with it. That's how I've survived so much crap in life. I would probably be living in a box somewhere if I didn't throw myself into the hard work of being better. You don't go from trailer parks to red carpets without a few (hundred thousand) tears and some cheap heels at classy parties. It's a process, but you can SLAY THE FAME GAME. And, as pre-tongue-obsessed Miley Cyrus would say, it's all about the climb.

The only way to climb the ladder of success with on- or offline fame, without going a little (or a lot) CRAY, is to make the commitment right now. Like, literally, right now ... Commit to growth and become the very best you can be. As a human and as a star.

Fame won't bring happiness and acting like a psycho won't help you develop legit relationships. I highly recommend something Jeff Olson talks about in his **FAB** book, *The Slight Edge*. He encourages people to read ten pages of a self-help or business book daily. That's 3,650 pages a year. Yay! My calculator can do math! The point is, commit to growth and you will do better in this industry and in the world.

Credit Johnny Chicollo
Eva A Catherine

IT'S ALL ABOUT RELATIONSHIPS

Life is about enjoying the people and opportunities that come, so make sure you invest in the people you meet. If you catch yourself being rude, Bon Qui Qui style, take a second and find out why. Did they diss you? Are you feeling insecure or inadequate next to them? I don't care how much you resemble Ariana Grande, you'll never reach legit success on your own. So, let's skip to the part where you accept that the world didn't start spinning the day you were born, and there are people who make the difference in whether you skip or SLAY THE FAME GAME.

I have a pretty fabulous career and am super grateful for my success. Am I arrogant? Definitely not. Sometimes I get annoyed at my own shadow. But, I do enjoy what I've built. I have no idea how much further my career will go. Most days I'm in shock of some new, exciting development I didn't even see coming. But, the thing that keeps me from going cray is that I have amazing people around. I also laugh at myself when I (often) fail. I'm incredibly grateful for every event invite, epic meeting, and new #fan I connect with.

Success can be just as stressful as failure, if not more. As soon as you're trending or have booked that huge gig, you're stressing about how long it will last or how you will book the next one.

GET READY FOR SUCCESS

Here's the deal. There's no "arrival" in this industry. For every couple of million who tune into your hit TV show, there are a couple of billion who have never heard of you. You might as well go ahead and claim celeb status right now. Start seeing yourself as the successful, sweet, fabulous celeb you were born to be. The sooner you can start feeling confident, the greater your chance at success. Step on that red carpet with confidence. It is time to own your power and rock that high split, Queen. But always stay humble when your fashion ends up in Vogue. Just act all chill like, "*Oh, I'm in Vogue? Wow, what an honor. I had no idea!*"

... They don't need to know about the Google Alert that just pinged you. =)

Look, in case you haven't noticed, I'm not a doctor, and in case you haven't, listen to me like I am one. Either way, I'm going to save you a ton of drama by helping you avoid the annoying mistake of self-sabotage. Maybe it was all those self-help books (1,000 and counting) or the fact that I've been that self-sabotaging perfectionist at times. Who knows! Either way, I totally get the whole 'human brain' issues ... so I want to help you avoid one of the worst.

21

I've done coaching, therapy, positive affirmations, support groups, etc. I've tried pretty much every success tool I could get my hands on. But, since all that jazz has to be crammed in one book, I'm hoping you're a fast learner, so I can save you some cash and time on all that crap. Okay, it's not crap. Especially if you're lucky enough to get my Hollywood therapist, Dr. Kupper. I adore him and his scholarly brain. But, he's mine and you can't have him. Haha!

The point is, self-sabotage sucks—so listen up ... You've seen it a million times with so many celebs, even if you aren't familiar with the term. In fact, if I had known I would end up in Hollywood, where the majority of people are crazy, I probably wouldn't have worked as hard on self-improvement.

Credit: Hamid Moslehi

If we're being honest (which we are), I could have been cray and still slayed. Fortunately for you, I didn't stop there ... so you can thank me later.

Rolling my eyes at myself.

I digress. The point is, self-sabotage is basically what people do when they are uncomfortable with success. You know, they get into fights, get arrested, spend all their money, act crazy, punch photogs, etc.

Unfortunately for them, there isn't a sabotage-o-meter to warn them when they are bombing their life ... so they just keep doing it. Doesn't it suck that we can't always spot our crazyville? Because we KNOW everybody else can. Although celebs have tons of loyal people hanging around, pitching tents in our vajayjays, and waiting for handouts; there's a point when brands and smart people start to back (or, often times, run) away. But who can blame them? It's actually the smartest thing they can do. However, it makes the crazies of the world implode that much faster. It's really sad, actually. So, if that isn't reason enough to stay healthy and connected to your family and real friends, I don't know what is! Also, be a good human and volunteer. And list three things you're grateful for every day. You're welcome.

Don't be like the majority of people who never change. Or, the one who waits until she bombs (AKA her career has an R.I.P. stone above it) to change. I know of many people in the industry who had amazing opportunities and careers, but couldn't take direction, acted like divas or were just mean. Needless to say, they aren't working anymore. This is a very small industry. Don't let the insane traffic or millions of social media accounts confuse you. The majority of the legit people in the industry all know each other ... and they know about crazies. I could kiss and tell, but I only have so much time before I head to the movies, so just don't get crazy, and you should be good.

Credit: Britt Barrett

GET COMFY IN THE UNCOMFY

If you're going to take on the challenge of making headlines and becoming a self-made fame Queen, you've got to get comfortable in the uncomfortable. People are going to judge you. They are going to annoy, hate, love, laugh at ... the list goes on. Basically, it's like high school × millions. But, of course, I was the nerdy homeschooled kid, so you're on your own with that one. Haha! I'm just kidding. I totally get the feeling of rejection and all the reasons you may want to fly under the radar or be perfect so no one judges you. However, dumbing yourself down isn't going to make insecure people feel any better about themselves. All it will do is stunt your own growth. So, get comfy in the uncomfy because life is about improving and evolving, and that doesn't always feel that great at first. So, don't get weird or boring to fit in with the not-so-fabulous people in your life. Get more fabulous friends.

AGING IN HOLLYWOOD
GULP

Focus TV

Speaking of uncomfy. I'll say, in this rando segue; it is pretty annoying to have to look cute *all* the time. I'll share tips to slay your style in Chapter four, but right now, I just need to vent. There's tons of unrealistic pressure to look hot on the daily in the industry. Most people will tell you that you need to make this a part of your brand. "Most people" includes me. But it is still annoying sometimes when you just want to look like a little hobo behind closed doors. Sure, I would never walk a carpet like that, but is it too much to ask for a non-makeup day (or week), comfy clothes, and a messy (like, truly messy) bun? Gosh, give a girl a break every now and then.

When I was defining my brand, I tried owning the "girl-next-door" vibes. One who doesn't have to look *that* cute all the time, but can just smile right through it. Unfortunately, I then discovered this weird vein that goes down the middle of my forehead. Wonderful. Just great. I can't even slay that approachable look. If you haven't seen it yet, please don't look too closely. Trust me, it's there. I've studied enough of my red carpet photos to notice it. People think I have a b**chy resting face. Nope. I'm just trying to keep that freaking vein at bay.

It's a never-ending game of dominoes. The whole reason I have that stupid vein is because I had to start getting Botox and crap. Apparently, I have a very expressive face, and it doesn't look great during photoshoots. Gosh, what happened to me? Apparently, as soon as you hit 22 in Hollywood, you're an old hag. No, I'm not 22, I just wanted to say that to mislead you. Whatever. Stop staring at me. I'm in my 20s, okay?! But who cares? I've decided to accept and slay every age. Sure, it may feel awkward at times. Blah. BUT, our thoughts need to be our BFFs. We need to love and accept ourselves. We shouldn't stress about a few lines on our foreheads ... worse case scenario, that's what Botox is for!

Speaking of which ... I'm told the key to getting Botox is never letting anyone in on your pointy little secret. Wonderful. Just great. So, basically, I have to CHOOSE to have these little needles pushed through my face, right next to my eyeballs, and I can't even vent about it to every random person I meet? Well, except for that poor, unassuming Uber driver who got me there? This is ridiculous. All this effort just to pretend I didn't do anything at all, so I can play off that whole 'looking youthful' crap. Aging might be the most unavoidable thing in the world, but God help me if I am going to go down without a fight. *"No really, please God, will you help me manifest the Benjamin Button syndrome? Thank you."*

24

Never mind, I said I was going to accept and slay every age, and I'm starting now. Thanks for listening to that therapeutic Rachel Rant though. I realize that it wasn't the most helpful to anyone here but me, so thank you. Now, you can add "philanthropist" to your social media bio. Plus, you get a peek at just how insane this business really is. Or, maybe you just think I'm insane. I personally think I'm making very sane responses to very insane situations. But let's move on. I don't want you sitting over there judging me.

Credit: Hamid Moslehi

WHAT'S YOUR WHY?

Before we go on, you need to figure out your why. You have got to have some very legit reasons why you want to be famous. I mean, aside from the fact that everyone pays attention to you, gives you prezies, and invites you to all the best parties. Oh, are those your only reasons? Okay. No judgment (at least none I care to admit). But, you're going to need something bigger to ground you. The sooner you know your why, the easier this industry will be. The fame game can be super hard. You'll blink and find yourself working nonstop wondering why you left Georgia in the first place—Oops! Did I trail off for a second? Maybe that's just me.

Lord (and my puppies) knows I have found myself on many a beach in Santa Monica wondering what the heck I'm doing out here. Why I'm working so hard and what my purpose is. I didn't realize then what I know now ... what my "why" really was. Writing a book called *SLAY THE FAME GAME* doesn't exactly lend itself to the self-help world (without throwing people off a bit), but I really do have a big heart for you.

I started my community in Hollywood, The McCord List, because I have hundreds of friends in the business who, even though they work as successful actresses, models, actors, and TV hosts, still struggle to deal with this crazy business. Helping them is my "why." I truly believe I'm helping the world. That purpose grounds me and helps me stay on point. Knowing your why is **EVERYTHING**.

This business is not for the faint of heart. Whatever that means. All I know is that I've personally thrown in the towel a million times. But I know my purpose is to help people, and I'm starting with this industry. I realize I'm a sassy choice for the self-help selection at the bookstore, but that's just me. Loubies and all!

I understand the insecurities and all that weird judgment as you shoot that slew of selfies. I probably shouldn't admit to it, but I get it. Bottom line, when you're dealing with rejection, embarrassment or annoyance in this business, you need to remember who you are and why you do what you do.

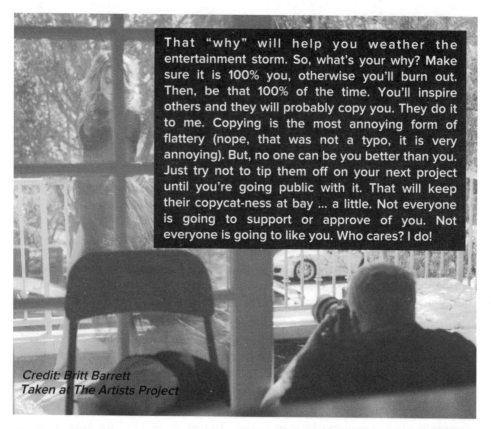

That "why" will help you weather the entertainment storm. So, what's your why? Make sure it is 100% you, otherwise you'll burn out. Then, be that 100% of the time. You'll inspire others and they will probably copy you. They do it to me. Copying is the most annoying form of flattery (nope, that was not a typo, it is very annoying). But, no one can be you better than you. Just try not to tip them off on your next project until you're going public with it. That will keep their copycat-ness at bay ... a little. Not everyone is going to support or approve of you. Not everyone is going to like you. Who cares? I do!

Credit: Britt Barrett
Taken at The Artists Project

Don't do this for the likes and comments, SLAY THE FAME GAME because it gives attention to a passion that fulfills your purpose. Be willing to make sacrifices (even if that means taking selfies e'ryday ... yes, I spelled that like the song) to make your dreams happen! You have to be so 100% sold on what you are doing. Be obsessed and grateful for every chance to fulfill your why!

CHAPTER 3
LET'S DO THIS ALREADY
Create Your Brand

Credit: Malachi Banales

This industry takes a lot of hard work. Anyone who tells you otherwise is probably insane, so you should back away ... slowly. But as hard as it might be, if you focus on getting a fabulous community of supportive, nonjudgmental friends, know your why, and develop a brand you're proud of, it can be pretty amazing!

Everyone in the industry is pursuing a dream; dreams of being actors, models, social stars, filmmakers, etc. Sure, they might take weird detours, but it's exciting to go for it in life. It demands you to be present, in tune, and leaned in. If you ever start to lose heart or feel lame, remember that most people never pursue their dreams. You're going for it! That's a big deal. Be freaking proud of yourself! One of my favorite people, Erwin, of Mosaic Hollywood, once said, "*The worst athlete is better than the best bystander.*" So true, right?

Even if you only bought this book to laugh at the industry (don't worry, I laugh all the way down my Instagram feed), make sure that whatever career you choose, you do it with passion. With your whole heart. Vogue features might not be in your future, but whatever is, give it passion, resilience, and gratitude.

Okay, enough of the cheesy for a minute, let's create your brand! Once you decide to go for it, you need to define who you are and what that means as a brand. Yes, you're a brand. Like it, live it, love it. Whatever you do, get used to it. Your journey to becoming a brand has already started—long before you realized. It is a combination of your natural talents, personality, passions, looks, choices, and favorite things all coming together. Cool, right? Not that anyone says "cool" anymore, but you get the point. Your brand is the marketable version of who you organically are.

That is what creating a successful brand is all about. It's a natural progression. I didn't know, when I first moved to Hollywood and started living this insane life, that one day I would write a book to help people SLAY THE FAME GAME and not break in the process. Yet, there I was, learning all about the industry and having a heart for the anxiety, brokenness, and depression that seem to go hand in hand.

If you start paying attention to who you are, every little step will soon make sense. Don't stress about the little fails in life. Breakups and missed opportunities will all make sense in the end. I wish someone would have told me that every seemingly stupid, embarrassing, stressful or pointless mistake would have led me right into this Sunset loft with a man I love and with Giggles and Munchkin, who are currently sleeping on every random inch of my boney body. Oh, and that I would one day be living fabulous life doing what I love. Gosh, if they had, I could have relaxed my Type A personality a bit.

This is me, telling that to you, so take a breath. You're creating a brand and building your future. You might not realize it yet, but you are! That means that every time you meet someone new, you have the opportunity to share a little more of your story, and see what that experience teaches you. Every stage can be exciting, especially when you understand your brand, and are constant 100% of the time. For example, if you want to be a dancer, you should be posting videos of your work, dressing like a dancer, and sharing your journey. Anything that fits within the filters of your brand as a dancer.

I'll share some exercises and tips to identify your brand, but no one can do it for you. You have to be the one to tune into your passion, focus and do the hard work (behind the scenes), and then stay glam and entertain. Understanding your brand is the first step because it shows you the strategy and direction you should be heading. If you want to be in fashion, you should be sharing trends and styles on your blog or social. Maybe you're an actress whose career isn't as hot as it was (that is TOTALLY normal, by the way. Don't be down on yourself ...). Just get it back up! Reinvent yourself. Start identifying some brands, and become their brand ambassador.

It's important to define your brand and work at it constantly. People can't see the talent that doesn't exist (duh). You have to work and grow every day. But don't want to wait until you're "perfect" to put yourself out there ... because you'd be waiting, umm, quite a while. Get out there and try some stuff. See what you think. Keep iterating until you find that perfect spot. If you do the work, create the content, build the fan base, you'll SLAY THE FAME GAME.

Credit: Britt Barrett

All I can do is teach you about this industry, tell you what works and what doesn't, and guide you with great resources. The rest is up to you. You have to be smart. You have to stay humble and always be grateful for everything. Even after you get your career off the ground, you have to keep at it. The hustle for Hollywood is real. It might be entertainment (and VERY fun at times), but it is still a business. Do what you say you will, stay focused, slay your style, get press talking, take classes, go to the right events, and build lasting friendships.

Credit: Tasia Wells

No one taught me how to SLAY THE FAME GAME. I've been figuring it out one fab or fail at a time. I would have loved it if someone had coached me. Hell, while I'm placing my "I wish" order at the "life counter," I wouldn't have minded all this coming a little sooner and with a lot less headache. But this is the industry I chose. If you can choose any other industry to be passionate about, do it. But, if not, just jump in and figure out your brand. And remember, every time I've tipped the paps to take my picture, and felt like some cheap skank afterward, I've been paving the way for you ... What? I didn't say I was Saint Rachel over here. I'm not a brain surgeon, I'm a celeb.

FAB EXERCISE TO DEFINE YOUR BRAND

My favorite exercise for developing a brand is to individually ask three close friends to help you come up with twenty to thirty, one to two word adjectives, to best describe you. Write each one down and put them aside. I love using Post-Its for this. An example of some could be: *beautiful, actress, model, inspiring, fabulous, classy,* etc. Next, individually ask three people who don't know you very well.

In fact, this would be the perfect activity if you have a couple people who have been wanting to hang with you for a while, but you haven't had the time. Have them come up with the same list, from their perspective. You need them to be honest and share what they see. Don't get defensive, if you don't like it. Just go with it. You can always complain about them behind their back later. OH, MY GOSH! Why am I not hitting backspace on that horrible advice? Obvi, don't try that last part at home.

Once you have everyone's notes, add in another five. But these should be attributes you aspire to. Maybe you aren't there yet, but that is the vision for your future.

Next, narrow your list down to five total. That's right, only five. You need to let some things go to focus hardcore on the best. Then voila! You should have what we call 'brand filters'!

WHAT'S YOUR NATURAL TALENT?

If you had a hard time with the above, don't worry! I recommend doing it twice, once at the beginning and once at the end of this chapter. Some of the questions that come up might help you figure it out. For example, what are you talented at and passionate about? Is it 100% you? Don't be afraid to be honest with yourself. You need to be self-aware and nonjudgmental. What random talents do you have that could be the perfect blend of a brand? Stay flexible when defining your brand. You might be amazed at the organic strengths you have for business that will do wonders for you. From networking skills to being fearless, be open to exploration. Don't commit to anything, just test some stuff out. It might make zero sense right now, but just keep reading and having fun with it.

The purpose is to identify who you naturally are and how you can put that into product form. You need it to be a brand people can connect with. Don't try and be someone you aren't.

Credit: Kelly McKeever

If you're naturally a Miley Cyrus, you would be wasting precious time trying to fit into an Adele mold. Let it go *Frozen* style, and be honest with yourself. If you want to be a little Disney princess, don't create rock music.

To SLAY THE FAME GAME, people need to be able to associate you with something. Great branding is key to being first in mind when people need someone just like you!

Why do you want to be famous? Do you love traveling?

Are you a foodie? If so, why not be a better version of Rachel Ray?

Are you into fashion? Get into modeling, fashion designing, blogging, or fashion curating.

Are you passionate about a human, animal, or environmental issue? Become a philanthropist.

Credit: Britt Barrett

If you don't brand yourself, someone else will ... and you might not like what they come up with. When you decide on your brand, you need to commit to it, Lady Gaga style. Otherwise, you'll come across as boring and unmemorable. And, the worst thing for a Queen would be to be basic. You need to get people talking and keep them talking. That will only work if you slay your brand ... over and over again. Think Madonna. She is the Queen of reinvention. If she weren't, we wouldn't be talking about her right now.

SHOW YOUR HEART

When developing your brand, you need to own all parts of yourself, but focus on the likable ones. What? It's true! I was recently helping a friend with advice for her brand. In doing some research into her social media insights, we learned that only 7% of her fanbase were women. That means that majority of the women who came across her page just kept going. Not a good ratio, especially for brand deals. Marketing executives love reaching women. But, from looks of her stats, she couldn't help them with that. Marketing execs are important because they have access to brands, and brands have dolla, dolla bills. You know the creators who "sell out" and actually pay their bills? That's called being a business BOSS. You need to go ahead and get comfy with it.

Anyway, my friend is gorgeous and has a super sexy brand. The problem was that women didn't like her ... at all. It made sense. She had been posting only lingerie pics. But, she is smart, and was open to changing up her posts to stay diverse and reach women on a heart level. So, we started to talk about why she did that. It was then that I learned she used to struggle with an eating disorder. Suddenly, it all made sense. She used to hate her body, and would literally injure it, in hopes of being lovable. Now, she is healthy and loves every inch of herself.

When someone survives something that intense, turns their life around like a Queen, and stuns with their gorgeousness, don't you think that should be celebrated? I believe in my friend's heart—and her Tyra Banks level of fierceness. Today, she is writing a book, and is on her journey to help other girls love themselves inside and out. Oh, and it doesn't suck that she is now growing her female audience, instead of alienating herself from them.

31

So many people, after a small dose of success, start to act like DIVAs. I should be honest, I tried it one day, but even I got tired of myself. It didn't fit who I am as a person. I'm a nerdy homeschooler who can't do one entire photoshoot without a goofy face (or twelve). My brand is me. Every part! Which doesn't include an overly diva side. Although, sometimes the way I share my opinions gets me in trouble sometimes ... oops! That's another story, but I am trying to keep that beach ball down!

Credit: Britt Barrett

That being said, I'm a little over-the-top. I am literally writing this chapter wearing an evening gown. Was I planning it? Of course not. I just felt like being a little over-the-top fabulous today. Plus, I just got back from an event and didn't want to change. When developing a brand, there are parts you should scale back on and parts you should amplify. Just don't be afraid to try new things as you brand yourself.

Most people don't consider fame Queens creative. I know, dumb. I judge them ... quietly. Which basically means, I give them a nice, condescending smize and continue on my way. After all, I know that we are the best creatives around. Have you ever seen our Instagram feeds? No, really, do you follow me yet? I really need you to do that. The higher my fan count, the better I feel about myself. JK! But, I still wanna' be BFFs. Follow me @iamRachelMcCord. I mean right now ... I will wait. =)

********BRIEF PAUSE FOR FOLLOW, STALK & LIKES********

Thank you, I needed that. Now, where were we? Ah, our Instagram feeds. Have you noticed how amazing our feeds are? Well, mine could use some more work, but I'm busy. In my head it's perfect. Anyway, most of us have amazing Instagram feeds. There are strategic themes, high maintenance color palettes, and plenty of posed candids to keep you thoroughly entertained ... or at least laughing. If that is not creative, I don't know what is. We care an embarrassingly lot about how things look and how many likes, comments, and hearts we get. But others would too if they had to work this hard to look good for a flat lay, that won't generate revenue and will get lost in your feed in two hours. It's exhausting ...The struggle is real, but fabulous. At least that's what I keep telling myself, as I go into a coma every night after a day of four events, five meetings, and a few photoshoots.

RECOGNIZE THAT CELEB BRAND

When you think of your favorite celebrities, you might realize that they each have their own brand. It might be hard to define at first, but once you learn to identify it, it will become obvious. When you choose your brand/title, make sure it's interesting and press worthy. For example, producer is more interesting than entrepreneur and model/author is more interesting than just an author. You have to find your sweet spot, and (hopefully) have the experience to back it up.

Now let's think of Katy Perry and Lady Gaga. They are super easy to define because their brands are hardcore in your face. Katy is the over-the-top emoji style pop star, while Gaga is the eccentric, wild woman who slays the shock factor—which makes every outlet cover her. But when you think about the Justin Timberlakes, Angelina Jolies, Jennifer Lawrences, and Jessica Albas of lala land, and it can get a little more confusing.

Below are the brand filters I would use to describe the following celebs:

Jennifer Lawrence: nails the girl-next-door, laugh at yourself dork vibes. As she also happens to sell out at the box office and stumble her way up the steps to nab awards.

Justin Timberlake: funny, southern boy from Tennessee who reinvents himself and sound frequently enough to stay relevant and current.

Angelina Jolie: private, A-lister humanitarian who cares more about human rights issues than what event she is attending tonight. Although she slays every red carpet like a QUEEEEN.

Jessica Alba: leveraged a small acting career to become a successful celeb entrepreneur, by serving the emerging market of eco-friendly, health conscious moms with her brand, The Honest Co.

Now think of some words that define and describe you. Can you create, or identify a brand for yourself that is truly natural to who you are? Can you create a short blurb like the ones above? Does it describe a likeable person who appeals to the masses? You want to stay down-to-earth, charming, and still entertaining. Remember this industry is all about charisma. Good luck, Queen!

Credit:
Alphie
Chikwashi

CHAPTER 4

SLAY YOUR STYLE: Trend in Press

This business is all about appearances. When you walk into a room, any room, you have got to be standing tall, ready for that close-up, okay?! Don't shy away from always looking like a celeb, BUT staying very nice in the process.

Credit: Malachi Banales

Just last week, I got delightfully overdressed (my fav way to be), and attended an event. As I arrived, the paps outside went insane. I couldn't tell if they recognized me or were just crushing on my outfit. Either way, I wasn't hatin'. Turns out, thanks to my overdressed, underpaid look, Daily Mail did an entire spread about my style and my work in Hollywood! The 3rd one that week! Can you hear me clapping and jumping up and down? No? Good.

Who knows if my favorite Daily Mail writers (like the fabulous Jabeen Waheed) will get tired of me. The best thing I can do is keep showing up, being kind, serving that SLAY, and happy dancing over every article.

While it's easy to celebrate a huge magazine spread, what about the days when you aren't feeling the SLAY? When people are giving you (and your style) the side glare with an extra cup of haterade? That sucks. If you were feeling ANY amount of insecurity over that frizzy hair or fashion you just threw together, this moment can really send you down a negative free fall. You have two options: 1) you can laugh it off and love every inch of yourself (duh) or 2) try the knee-jerk "*You can't hurt me*" vibes, resulting in you becoming the biggest DIVA in the room so your feelings aren't hurt. I'm hoping you always choose the first option. I have a fun way of dealing with haters anyway, just keep reading …

I dealt with that side glare recently when I left a Beautycon party in a fun, girly outfit for a *very* serious Vanity Fair event. It was SO awkward. I walked up in my tight pants, over the knee boots, crop top, and Ariana Grande pony, just as Selma Blair graced the red carpet in this posh Chanel suit. We all know she has had her, ahem, less posh, more airport crazy moments, but still. Can you hear my entry brakes?! I already struggle to fit in with vibes like that, but in this case, with this outfit, I had zero chance of fooling anyone of my poshness. I think my entire outfit cost $45. You're welcome, wallet. I'm sorry judgers.

Credit: Stephanie Girard

By the way, I love my inexpensive looks. They are kind of my go to. Still, I was feeling wayyyy underdressed, which was unusual. So, I did what any sane person would do ... I Ubered the hell outta there, changed at my house (fortunately, just a few blocks away from this Chateau Marmont event), came back, and ended up in a bunch of press saying how "put together my look was." Haha! If they only knew how NOT put together I felt. I mean, if by "put together" they meant: a five-minute panic attack, tornado in my closet, finished off by having to center my entire outfit over the need to cover up boot marks on my legs... Sure! You're absolutely right. I was, ahem, "put together."

No one is exempt from fashion insecurity in Hollywood or on social media. We are all nervously dressing for that red carpet or social post. But it's time we face our fears and open mouth laugh poise our way through events (even when all we want is to crawl under a blanket in front of our Netflix happy place).

Besides, worst case scenario, you end up on the wrong side of the, "Who Wore It Better" list. There are worse things in the world. I've been pitted against Carmen Electra and Kim Kardashian, and I only lost with one of them. Yay! Besides, if you use these crazy tips and take some calculated risks, chances are you'll be a fashion pro in no time. Don't stress. I can tell you from personal experience that I don't have any regrets. Okay, that's not true ... at all. But it did sound mature, didn't it? Okay, here's the truth ... most of my regrets are for NOT putting myself out there. That is except for one outfit that I still cringe over today. It was AWFUL! Silver dress, black faux fur, tights, and a little nausea for the innocent bystanders ...

... trails off in stupidity ...

Now, let's get you on the slay game. To get started, I highly suggest dumping out every single item from your closet and all your drawers. Don't leave anything in. Throw them across the room, hell the entire house. This is what it will look like by the time you leave for events anyway, so you might as well get a head start. Hollywood standards are ridiculously high. Are you ready? Me neither, but we might as well get this over with.

Credit: Adam Kay

LA CHIC

It's time to get your wardrobe "LA-inized." I realize it isn't technically a word, but what am I? A professional author or something? Oh, wait ... Who cares! I need that word because it perfectly describes how people change when they move out here. All the sudden, they talk raspy, buy their first leather jacket, start showing up late, wearing sunglasses inside, etc. The point is, they start picking up the celeb-meets-hipster style of the city. I think it's great. It is definitely an upgrade from the khakis and polos they probably wore in middle A (America). I love that cute little clean-cut look, but it isn't very LA. I mean, just check out my hubs (@RickSchirmer) if you ever want to see how I think men should dress. He is the hottest. Mic drop.

The style for meetings, castings and casual events is what I call 'LA chic'. Clearly, I've become LA-inized. LA chic is when you wear a fun, casual, form-fitting dress with heels, fab jewelry and glamorous shades. You could also slay LA chic with some leather leggings or tight jeans, knee high boots and, again, some sick jewelry. To me, sick jewelry means more gold rings than a Queen, big hoops or long chandelier earrings, drape necklaces and trendy bracelets. Not all at once ... obviously. Eek. That would be a disaster! If you're doing a necklace, skip the ears (unless you've got those diamond studs), or just do earrings, a bracelet, and rings. Oh, and sunglasses matter. A lot. If you're like me, you'll have a couple diva pieces from Prada and Louis Vuitton, but you'll score most of your collection at $10 a pop at a cute boutique or, if you're in Hollywood, from Venice (which is a little too hipster for me ... well, with the smell of pee on the streets and all).

Credit: Adam Kay

Please remember that a two-piece suit would be the death of your talent career. You basically need to put your professional clothes in one of those weird vacuum bags under your bed, because unless you give up on the fame game anytime soon, you won't be rocking those that much on social or in Hollywood. Although, this week my man and I did have a meeting with the incredible Dr. Phil and his stunning wife, Robin McGraw. Let's just say I had to steam those pencil skirt wrinkles four times and shake off (a lot of) dust. Speaking of which, make sure you pick up a steamer, it's a random but real tip. If you don't already have one, you could score the little $25 travel one from Bed Bath & Beyond. That is what I have. But, no judgment if you want to get all fancy with a crazy big machine ... that is, if you want to surrender ⅛ of your apartment. That's on you. I'm not judging. Okay, I'm judging a little ... no, more accurately, I'm judging a lot.

OKAY! I'M DONE

TRENDS

The most important strategy for style, regardless of your brand filters, is to make sure your looks grab attention. Not because you wore some crazy beef filets or a swan on your chest, but because they are gorgeous and different. Your looks need to stand out. These tips can help you grab attention from press editors:

- Be over-the-top fashionable
- Go weird, eccentric, or different
- Show some skin, if age appropriate (but not too much—keep it classy)
- Hug your curves in all the right places
- Be dramatic
- Do something different
- Catch a trending color
- Wear something really ugly (I obviously don't like this one)
- Dress like another celeb
- Wear something current / controversial

If the above freaks you out because you usually sit in the corner at events, waiting to leave or hoping no one is paying attention to you, you're at the wrong party. Hell, the wrong industry. In this industry, when you walk into a room and every eyeball is on you, that's a good thing. That doesn't only matter in Hollywood. If you're a social media queen in Ohio, you still need to stand out.

When I used to practice my catwalk with my sisters in the Mall of Georgia, I cannot tell you how many people would stare, drop their jaws, get annoyed, etc. The point is, we were getting people to pay attention. It seems so obvious, but in the entertainment industry you actually have to be entertaining. **BOOM.** Biggest revelation of the book ... so far. You're welcome.

Credit: Alphie Chikwashi

Don't worry if you aren't Taylor Swift (if you are, umm ... hey girl, heyyyyy), you are YOU! Don't waste that talent trying to be someone else. Your style needs to feel organic and natural to you! It's great to trend in the press, but only if it is on your terms, in something you're comfortable with. If you are into it, yay! It's time for your hotness to run this city. It can be hard to rise (or, more accurately, elbow your way) to the top, so just release that annoying perfectionism that makes you so scared to fail, look dumb, or feel stupid. That crap is inevitable so just let it go. Feel it, then use that mascara wand to wave it off like the Queen you are!

STOP FIDGETING, YOU LOOK FAB

You need to bring your most fabulous self to every shoot. Your portfolio (aka your book/social media channel) is only as strong as your weakest look, so capture and use the best possible photos. That means make sure your dresses fit perfectly (or pin them), your makeup is flawless, you have nothing in your teeth, and your hair is on fleek. Also, make sure you practice your poses in front of the mirror in every outfit before you go out. You need to make sure you're capturing the best angles. Also, tape down, cover up, or pack in anything you don't want popping out! I'm obsessed with nipple covers, fashion tape, and the occasional band to give me a waist on a dress that would otherwise be too flowy.

Once you've put the time in and rubbed in that last drop of gloss, step away from that vanity; it is time to own the look and STOP fidgeting. You look fab. Just like you just did five minutes ago. Commit to your gorgeous and WALK ... AWAY. Don't mess with your hair all night. Just pin the flyaways so you can focus on that pearly white smile for the cameras. Once you have your look, you need to be comfortable. You aren't going to be perfect. But, you can be perfectly you! If you put the proper thought into all the details, you already slay!

One thing to remember, if you aren't getting all the compliments you deserve, is that some people are too busy worrying about themselves to notice how flawless you look. Just be your fabulous self and validate yourself. ** Bonus points when you choose to go ahead and (genuinely) compliment them.

Who cares if they don't return the favor and say how fab your legs look ... have YOU seen them? We all know they are perfect!

I have a girlfriend who was having a hard time recently. We went to lunch together to catch up and I could tell right away that she wasn't in a good place. She had been working with a new manager who was always putting her down and the worst part was that she was starting to believe him. It showed on her face, in her style and the way she carried herself. You may think that no one notices, but they do. Beauty comes from the inside. So, what you think about yourself is a BIG deal. Confidence truly is your best accessory! You don't belong on the sidelines. If someone makes you feel less than, let them go.

You can't surround yourself with crappy people and things that bring you down. The people you surround yourself with will affect every part of your life, from photo shoots to meetings to castings, etc. If you're going to build a lasting career in this industry, you need to have the energy to shine—so don't hang with people who pull you down. Oh, and if you need to skip the blowout bar for a little therapy session, DO IT, QUEEN!

Credit: Britt Barrett

You also need to protect what you believe about yourself. You need your thoughts to build you up. If you notice your thoughts turning on you, just say, "*STOP*" out loud (hopefully when you're alone). Startle yourself into thinking positive thoughts about yourself and others.

I got papped by some photographers yesterday and the photos went on a bunch of press sites. Of course, I decided to read the comments, because that's what you should do ... never. Apparently, I have a "great body and ugly face." That's fine, we can cover more of that in my haters section ... where they belong. But, do you think I'm going to let a few nameless trolls get me on a negative track? Umm, hi, no. Not a freaking chance. Neither should you. You're beautiful inside and out. You think Rebel Wilson isn't called fat? Or Anna Kendrick weird looking? Sure, I do realize I'm using A-listers for comparison, but it's my book. I can do what I want. The point is, don't believe the negative crap out there and DEFINITELY don't start telling yourself those hateful things!

WERK IT

Whatever you wear, when you hit that red carpet or social media feed, be ready to pose away in that gorgeous look. Oh, and don't be fooled, it takes skill to take these photos. Most people take photos with an awkward forward lean, head tilt, and hands on the hip. Oh, and don't get me started about their over-excited smile (I do it ALL the time). Figure out your perfect poses, because unless you're Paris Hilton circa 2005 (aka you weren't born rich, so you have to self-park your car twelve blocks away), you have to slay those red carpets. I'm talking hair, makeup, posing, positive thinking … SLAY. Oh, and give yourself a pat on the back of that fabulous sequin jacket for giving it your best (even if you missed the mark). I already know you are SLAYING the game!

TRUST YOUR GUT

Credit: Stephanie Girard

You can protect your brand if you always trust your gut. If you're trying to look like a serious actor, don't have a "wardrobe malfunction." If you're trying to play up the A-lister swag, don't do a thousand selfies on the carpet … ever … even if this is your hottest outfit ever. Please, for the love of Queens everywhere: walk around the corner and get an artsy shot in a cool alley. Or, if you're like me, in your parking garage.

You don't have to spend a lot. I probably spent less than $4,000 on clothes last year … combined. I know, I can hear your gasps from here. I just don't shop that much. Sure, I'm gifted and loaned tons of stuff. But, I still wear stuff I've had for years. I just find that perfect accessory or piece to spruce up the look. It is easier than it seems. As long as it is on brand, I am happy!

Start studying fashion. Literally. Go on social media and check out the fashion hashtag. It isn't to encourage you to buy every item you see, it's just to help you hone in your creative eye and find styles that fit your brand. I spend a lot of time trying new things. I know that a pop of color must be done right to keep from looking like it got lost on its way to another outfit. You have to test things out little by little. You'll make mistakes (we all do) but that's okay! I wish I could go in your closet and pull looks together for you … That would be so much fun! But don't worry, you got this! Just ALWAYS trust your gut!

When I was shooting the cover for this book, I styled myself (with the help of my FAB FAV, Aaron from Ivan Bitton Style House) in a GORG $20,000 dress I pulled. I picked all the accessories, but, like a magnet, I kept wanting to try this big, tulle black dress. I ended up ignoring my gut and sticking with the other one. Umm, until the next morning when I had my assistant pull the one I was obsessing over! Of course, THAT was the one we shot. I'm so happy I listened to one of my best friends and photographers, Britt Barrett. I know it seems like such a small thing but when you're a creative and have a specific concept in mind, you *have* to push for it. Even when everyone else doesn't understand.

DON'T BE BASIC WITH YOUR CELEB STYLE

To help you slay, I'm sharing some tips on what you could wear, if you fit in the following celeb categories:

Katy Perry: If you're the fun, goofy girl in the room, be open to try some over-the-top, fun outfits that capture your attitude and grab attention. Have fun, be colorful, and keep it YOU.

Adele: If you want to be viewed as the classy, serious celeb you are, you can go the Adele route. She is more conservative, but always fabulous. For this look, dress for your shape, show off your best assets, and opt for the more dramatic options. Press loves big gowns that capture attention. If you're going the conservative route, make sure you nail it with drama.

Kim Kardashian: If sexy fits your brand and you're not afraid to show your body, this is your style. Sheer dresses that cover the necessities usually get picked up. I'm not recommending a boring cocktail dress from a random boutique (although you don't need to splurge to rock the carpet). Find something that stands out. This is your moment to get GLAM and be over the top. The point isn't to show TOO much. Wear what makes you feel comfortable, and rock it with a big smile. Oh, and DON'T make everything about you. You can still stay likeable and connect with everyone at the party, even when you look intimidating AF.

Lady Gaga: This look works if you're strong, fierce, and oh so outrageous. I truly believe that Lady Gaga blew up as big as she did because of her perfectly timed shocker outfits. That, paired with epic music and an amazing voice, makes her the total package. There are tons of incredibly talented artists, but without the ability to SLAY THE FAME GAME and get press cover you, you won't get very far in the traditional Hollywood side of the industry.

There are so many celeb styles to consider. Men and women. I don't study men's styles as much, but this is a start when determining where your brand fits. Study red carpet styles. Study Daily Mail, E! News, US Weekly, etc. Pay attention to the fellow fame Queens in the showbiz section. Why are they getting covered? What did they do that worked so well? What can you do similar that still fits your brand?

LAZY GIRL'S GUIDE TO GLAM

This industry can come with a lot of pressure to look Instagrammable at all times ... as stressful as that may be. A life in the spotlight, even if you only have fifty followers (so far), means you are committing to putting yourself out there ... a lot.

It makes it easier to capture content if you're always camera ready, even if you're only going on an

errand. Especially if you have other influencer friends (which you want), because they might whip out that iPhone and oh snap (literally), you'll be regretting you skipped that concealer.

My day "off" (you'll learn I never *actually* never takes days off, except Sunday for my faith) yesterday began with a DMV appointment. I know, I'm keepin' it classy. A girl's gotta do what a girl's gotta do! I was going to go looking pretty BASIC, but then I figured I might need a license photo, and since I'm a vain hoe, I couldn't be looking legit hobo, so I did a little something something ... what I like to call lazy girl's glam. After my appointment, I headed to the Grove (my fav place ever), and texted a girlfriend to join me.

Before long, my errand had turned into a full-on girly photoshoot, puppy date in the lawn. Which meant I was posting on my Instagram story where I was, so another friend texted me and joined. We had such a blast. Later that day, when a photographer recognized me and starting shooting (I first looked over my shoulder because I hadn't called them), all I could think was, "*thank goodness I did my lazy girl glam routine.*" The point is, you never know how your fabulous day will go, so you might as well dress and glam yourself in a way that makes you feel beautiful and ready for whatever excitement the day throws at you.

Don't worry, looking glam on the daily doesn't mean you need to sacrifice your peace of mind. Of course, there are also the days when you should just be makeup free as a bird (I also do this all the time), but for the days you aren't, you don't need to spend hours. I have some makeup hacks to keep a lazy girl glam on the daily.

The lazy girl's guide to makeup is all about maintaining that natural fabulousness of you. You don't need a Kylie eye to be beautiful. Natural beauty is one of the greatest things in my opinion. You have it, don't hide it. Sure, I could teach you about contouring and eye makeup, but, let's please be honest, that space is CROWDED with a capital "C". Just go on YouTube, take a deep breath and sneeze. At least 42 will pop right up. I need to stay little different.

So, I bring you: the lazy girl's guide to makeup. After spending 6 months respecting my Sundays and boycotting makeup, only to regret it 26 times (do the math on that) after running into people I know every time, I decided to find a happy medium. How could I give my skin a much-needed break and still feel beautiful?

The solution, aka the Rachel guide to lazy girl glam, came unexpectedly. I got a comp facial at Ciel SLS in Hollywood (the perks of my job don't suck) and they sent me an entire set of the Biologigue-Recherche skincare products. You know, the legit brands that you usually try to pretend you don't want after an hour and a half of facialists treating your skin and lecturing you about your 99 problems.

"Nah, I'm happy with my $4 Cetaphil cleanser, but thank you so much! I'm really ridiculously rich and just choosing to pass on that $3,000 set you pulled for me. Don't worry, I could easily carve that out of my budget, I'm just not interested. "

Anyway, for some reason, they decided to gift me with *everything*. I'm talking EVERYTHING. I went from washing my face with some good ole' Rite Aid goodness (no moisturizer) once a day, to an eight product process twice a day. That's right. I spend 2 of the 12 hours I'm awake each day, cleaning off the other 10 hours of my life off my face. Two cleansers, one toner, two serums, two moisturizers, and an additional eye cream my aunt created ... you know, just in case. I realize this seems excessive but to be honest, within one month of obsessing over my face (which required a huge life adjustment ... but, who cares, I didn't like working out during that time anyway), my face completely transformed. But, not like an episode of Botched, I'm talking about face glow you can see from space. In fact, my face is so clean these days it looks oily. I'm a germophobe, and I could literally eat off my left cheek it is so clean ... in fact, sometimes I do. Moving on ...

I realize that doesn't sound like a lazy girl's solution, but hear me out ... now that I spend more time and money (or Instagram shout-outs) on the health of my skin, I'm able to skip most of the makeup I relied on to feel beautiful. I didn't even realize how dull my skin looked before. Now, all I do is dot a little concealer (I use *NAR, Medium 1 in Custard*) under my eyes, add mascara, blush, and lip balm. Done and done. BOOM! Lazy girl's guide to glam.

Credit: Adam Kay

I know, I know, the stories took longer than the tip. But, that is the truth. The way you care for your body, heart, skin, and mind is SO important. Don't get so busy with the outside that you forget that beauty goes much further! Oh, and drinking lots of water basically helps everything.

SLAY THAT RED CARPET EVENT

When you're rocking a red carpet, it's no time for laziness. It's like the prom—this is your chance to prove to your neighbors that you aren't the homeless friend who lives down the hall. You are a gorgeous Queen ready to slay that carpet! To get you ready, there are a few things you need to know:

1) Remember how to find a YouTube makeup tutorial? Hop on and get to sneezing. I highly recommend trying out different looks long before you actually need to slay that carpet. Give yourself the chance to get better at it. Remember, makeup techniques will look different on you than other people. That's because of facial and eye shapes, etc. Be open to mixing and matching tips from different people. Try an eyeliner technique from one person and contouring from another. Some of my girlfriends who do awesome tutorials include: Sazan Hendricks, Teni Panosian, and Lynette Cenee.

2) Practice your red carpet poses in front of a mirror. I know it sounds incredibly cheesy, but it works. If you have no idea how to start, look up red carpet videos of Gigi Hadid or Angelina Jolie. They both slay.

3) Dominate the room. As soon as you walk in the room, the first thing everyone is thinking is, *"Who is that?"* Once you've made your entrance, meet them and tell them. Don't you dare crawl in the back with your shoulders hunched over like you just got scolded by your mama. You stand TALL, own that fab! You got this. You're beautiful! Just remember to smile and laugh.

4) Be kind. Don't be a snob. No one likes a snob. They have expiration dates. Be the super model show-stopper with a heart of gold. Assume that everyone is your best friend and treat them that way.

5) Access your assets. Look, no one has a perfect body, face and hair. Often, I look like a possum, but who cares if I have long legs or big hair (unless it is due for a wash) to overcompensate. Work with what you have. I swear, if I hear another Queen say she needs to lose weight, has a breakout, or is bloated when I compliment her, I just might shake her. YOU ARE GORGEOUS. Get it in your head and keep it there. No one can make you feel bad about you except you. They can point their fingers or make comments, but the feelings are inside your mind, which means you can choose to believe the crap or not.

CHAPTER 5

Credit: Britt Barrett

SLAY IT: Content Strategy

You need to constantly create content. You might not be getting endorsements yet, aka still doing tons of unpaid selfies, but that's okay. You still need to create consistent content to grow and engage your fan base ... even if you only have five fans. To keep up with all the OOTDs, MOTDs, etc., tripods, collaborations, and random people walking by will be your photographer friends right now. Sure, you may be getting tons of weird looks from your Instagram boyfriend or the innocent bystanders who bear witness to your pop-up iPhone shoots, but you won't regret it when you get that glam shot up on social media. We all know nothing says, "I'm not *really* famous" quite like a pop-up iPhone photoshoot, but we ALL do it ... last night in my garage to be exact.

No matter where you are in your career, you always need great content to stay connected with your fans. But don't worry, once you're really balling, you can splurge on a real camera or a free intern to follow you around all day and take your picture. Besides, before long, you might have the paps capturing you! But, let's not get ahead of ourselves. For now, let's start with your strategy.

WHAT TYPE OF CONTENT TO POST?

Now that you know who you are as a brand, it is time to tell the world. President Obama wrote his autobiography so he could educate the masses about who he was and what he valued. I mean, I've never read it, but that is what I've heard. If you want to be known for acting, you had better be posting stuff with you acting all the time. If you want to be known as a famous socialite, you had better be going out all the time and snapping photos of it. People will believe what you show them. That is why your strategy is so important. You don't want people looking at an Instagram about cats having no idea that you're an incredible writer. Share your heart.

My husband is a launch strategist. He founded LaunchPreneur, where he helps entrepreneurs and filmmakers launch their careers and projects. On his Instagram, he is constantly sharing tips and advice for entrepreneurs. That way, anytime anyone goes on his social, they know who he is and what he is passionate about. For me, I'm constantly sharing images of my press, modeling campaigns, and events. But I also love showing my heart ... my dogs, speaking engagements with teens, my friends, etc.

What do you want to be known for? My brand filters are: fabulous, positive, inspiring, well connected, philanthropist, events, red carpets, fashion, beauty, travel, etc. That means, every one of my photos needs to fit into those categories. Have you created your brand filters, yet? That's a trick question, I know you did. Now, let's do something with them. Do you have a great personality? Maybe video is right for you. Do you love modeling? Why not teach fashion styling or runway walks? Get creative. Makeup tutorials have been done ... and done AGAIN. But, if that is what you love, go for it! It needs to be organic to your passion so it can sustain itself. If not, you'll be fresh out of content by day three.

Credit: Britt Barrett

WHAT'S STOPPING YOU?

If you're going to slay this fame thing, you need to understand what's stopping you. For example, why do you hide from the cameras when you could be photobombing every random selfie to get your face out there? Okay, maybe that is a little extreme, but you get my drift. I hate being the girl who hogs the photogs at an event. But, there's one girl in Hollywood who would BFF it up with the janitor if it could get her into a party or on a carpet. We all have our reasons, but if you don't know what yours are, you might be in trouble!

A problem identified is half solved (as they say), so it is time to identify yours. I know it can be annoying ... seeing as how we're both so flawless ... but, hypothetically speaking, let's say you had a flaw ... what would it be? The most common is the fear of failure. What IF you start creating content and NO one engages with it?? Eek! That would be painful. No likes, no follows, no love. But, here's a thought ... what if they LOVE it! If you're being authentic and sharing an interesting point of view, people will watch and share. Besides, no one will engage with content you didn't create so you might as well give it a shot. BOOM! Big wisdom heard here first. I should write a book or something. Ha!

It's funny but true. Sure, you can sit there and think of a million reasons (Lady Gaga style) it won't work or you can just start creating, start doing. You can always iterate and evolve. But, you must at least start. Don't worry; it's possible and you've got this, but you have to figure out what is stopping you.

Credit: Alphie Chikwashi

WHAT'S HELPING YOU?

For every excuse, you also have resources just waiting to be used. And, since most people have tons of excuses, you probably have more resources that you realize. I mean personality, talent, time, passion, motivation, relationships, access, etc. There's nothing that turns my stomach more than hearing someone complain about their (lack of) career, followed by the breakdown of how they spent their day sleeping in, lying by the pool and partying until 2 a.m. Your career won't fall into your lap. You need to go grab it by the cajones.

Don't spend so much time looking at your "have nots" that you can't see your "haves." For example, writing this book is terrifying on every level, but the truth is, I'm incredibly connected in Hollywood. Not to be obnoxious, but, in all honesty, I am. From hosting events to intimate gatherings curating all the right people, it isn't really that hard for me to make things happen. In fact, with a recent photo shoot I did, my community was so supportive, we had a reach of over 596 million. I am #blessed. =)

The point is, it was still scary to believe in myself enough to go for it with my book. To share my advice with the world. I mean, was anyone *really* gonna care? The truth is, it wasn't until I started doing it and talking about it, that I realized there is a need for this. You have to choose to go for it. Use your gifts, knowledge, and resources to build the career you love. Then, pick up the phone and ask for support as you pursue your dreams. It's scary, but that's how it's done in this industry. Get vulnerable. Be bold. You won't make it if you don't just do it!

INNOVATE

The best films, shows, and projects are all ones that are different and new. If I watch another rom com with the "surprise ending" that the guy falls in love with the best friend who has been there all along, I might pull a few hairs out. Pleaseeeee. We all know how that will end. Nah, I want to be surprised. Taken off guard. The same goes for digital content. If you do OOTD shots like everyone else, you'll blend in like everyone else. Sure, it is super annoying when people copy you, but I would rather innovate with an amazing concept that results in people copying me, than settling as another one of the masses. It gets so boring.

Credit: Adam Kay

You need to innovate. Reinvent. Don't be afraid to think and be creative. Think outside the box. The layout of this book is a perfect example. I wanted something different so we created it. Watch what everyone is doing, then do something different. That is what Chick-Fil-A (one of my FAVs) does. That's why they SLAY the competition. That doesn't mean you throw out everything that works. Just challenge the norm a little. For example, everyone loves to post YouTube reaction or response videos because they get to ride the wave of a video going viral. It works. I get it. I've even personally experienced it. But, find a way to pull it back to content that supports your strategy and messaging. For example, just because a video of a mouse eating a block of cheese is going viral doesn't mean a beauty vlogger should do a response video. Otherwise, you'll end up with one million views from weird mouse lovers who give zero crap about eyebrows on fleek.

If you're funny, why not talk about your crazy journey to SLAY THE FAME GAME? Make fun of the process. Laugh and be silly. People love to see behind the scenes, especially if you're making fun of yourself and being silly along the way! You got this, I already know!

CREATE A PLATFORM

The entertainment industry is shallow AF. That means you need to be prepared to create a beautiful platform that really captures your brand. People can be HATERS (more on that later in the book), so you definitely want to spend some energy in the beginning WOWing your new fans. The way to do that is to take the time with design that makes you appear better than you are. 'Fake it till you make it' style. For example, if you're just starting out and don't have a lot of fans, you need to create the illusion that you're the biggest celeb, blogger, YouTuber, influencer out there. The way to do that is to step outside your brand and give it an honest up and down. Do you have a dedicated URL? Or is your website: www.wix.com/youknowyouloveme?

Whichever platform you choose: blog, social media platform, official website or YouTube, everything needs to be BEAUTIFUL (don't skimp on this). People may not know your name (yet) but if your platform is as memorable as your brand, you will get the invite, gig, and deal you're hoping for!

I was really lost when it came to designing my brand. I didn't know what or who I wanted to be. It took a while and a ton of mistakes to figure that out. You have to be patient with the journey and cut yourself a little slack as you figure it out. In case you're one of those results-oriented, let's get to the point types, you should start your deep breathing now. It is a process. Whether you need to shoot 50 videos, work with a bunch of website developers, or spend hours and hours on content, it is going to take a hot minute. Don't skip this. To get started, compare what you love from some sites and what you can't stand from others. The process takes time, fabulous design, amazing strategy, and lots of hard work. Slay your brand and everything else will fall into place. Skimp on this and you'll look as random as an outfit with red stripes, leopard print, and pink fur. You get the point ...

WHICH PLATFORM, THOUGH?

Choosing your platform is important. If you're hilarious, entertaining, have a great personality, are musically talented... video is going to be killer. Find the place you're the most talented and share it with the world. If you aren't *that* talented at video but do it anyway, you might end up with some painful comments and feedback. It's better to go in the direction that you are a Queen at. If you're gorgeous but a little video shy, modeling in still images could be a fabulous choice! Whatever you do, make sure it is something you naturally love and are willing to dedicate hundreds of free hours to. Nope, that was not a typo. You won't make money right away and you'll work NONSTOP.

If I had it my way, I would be Ariana Grande, workin' side to side, but my singing isn't *that* great. When I created my brand, I had to be honest with myself and lean on my natural skills for modeling and writing. That is why I chose to create a blog and use social media. I can always take singing lessons and get back into the studio, but the key was to build enough success that I could leverage it to open other doors I'm passionate about. That's how I got *"The Rachel McCord Show: From Trailer Parks to Red Carpets."* Knowing the direction you *plan* to go in helps you choose the right platform to create long-term success.

Do you know the end goal? If it is to be a successful actress, make sure your platform lends itself to video content so you can share clips of your work. Whatever you do now needs to be the small steps that take you in the direction of your end goal. The platform is your way of owning the audience and building a relationship with them that will outlast the social media platforms like Instagram, Snapchat, Facebook that eventually go away. Your platform is a website that houses all your videos, pictures, conversations, etc.

If we could all snap our fingers and make it happen, we would. But, if you want to be successful (duh, you do) you must be willing to do what unsuccessful people won't. Like right now, it's Saturday, I'm tired. I think I've already worked a sixty-hour week. I want to nap and chill, like my chihuahua who is snoring next to me. But, I need to be willing to take small steps to get closer to my dream. I am on the constant grind. The good news is that this business will work for you if you're humble enough to work at it. I've watched my brand rise, but I wasn't sitting down in a lounge chair as I did. I was head down, hardcore focused.

A beautiful thing happens when you create an epic platform and dedicate your time and energy to sharing fabulous content that makes people's lives better. You'll build a name and fame for yourself, and it will open up the doors to do the jobs that bring you the most joy. Maybe you love makeup, modeling, styling, entrepreneurship, or acting. If you can build the audience, you can build the dream. That's because the entertainment industry is all about money. Brands want to be involved in entertainment so they can get more eyeballs on their product, so they can sell more. If you build a fanbase and help brands reach the people who love you, you'll be able to do what you love as a career for a long time. If you can't create access to the audience and fans, you can't make money with brand sponsors. You would need to go the traditional way of auditioning until you get hired. But, if you have the audience, you have the power. That is what new media is all about.

Just remember, you're developing a platform to connect with and grow your fanbase. That is your number one objective. Once you do that, you can get paid to entertain, host, and connect with them. Some people could be waiting tables while pursuing their dreams part time, but I think it's more strategic to choose a day job that teaches you about social media marketing so you can quickly leverage those skills to grow your own platform fanbase. Then, you can pull in brand sponsors to help you make enough money to pay your bills as you build fame. We will discuss this more in the monetization chapter, but I'm on a flight right now sipping a yummy glass of pinot grigio. And to be clear, I didn't say "sipping a yummy glass of ..." to be annoyingly posh. I'm actually on an annoyingly turbulent flight and it is either a glass of wine or crying on this poor guy's shoulder to my right. I figured wine was a better choice. Besides, he is sandwiched between me and a human grizzly bear who is completely unfazed by the bumps, with his loud snoring rattling my brain ever since takeoff. And, yes, you're correct, I am in coach ... lifestyles of the humble.

GET STARTED

The first thing I always say about doing anything is that the most important part of anything is getting started. Don't doubt yourself, you're beyond fabulous. Don't be afraid that no one will like or follow. Even if you only ever encourage, inspire, help, or entertain one person, isn't that enough? Okay, maybe you would prefer more fans than your mom, but you need to believe in your passion so much that even if only one person is impacted, you know that they are worth it. When I started out, I knew it would be enough for me if I helped only five people truly go for it in life. The image of those five people mattered so much to me that all the work I would do to get there would be worth it. If I could help them avoid the casting couch or the BS of insecurities this industry serves you with a smile, I would be happy. Once I released my own ego of how big I wanted it to be, and realized how important my work was, I knew I was ready to go for it.

LET'S DO THIS ALREADY!

Now that you have a brand, know your content strategy, have that hair on fleek, and are ready to let go of your fear and start creating content; it is time to do it!

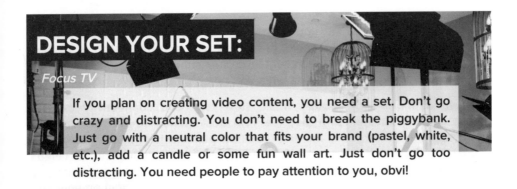

DESIGN YOUR SET:

Focus TV

If you plan on creating video content, you need a set. Don't go crazy and distracting. You don't need to break the piggybank. Just go with a neutral color that fits your brand (pastel, white, etc.), add a candle or some fun wall art. Just don't go too distracting. You need people to pay attention to you, obvi!

LIGHTING:

Lighting is super important. Fans get annoyed when the pixilation is off or the image is too dark. I used to hate flash on my iPhone, but when compared to images that look like they were shot in a dark alley, I learned how to fix those red eyes and move on. Natural lighting is the best. Try mornings or evenings for the perfect glow. If you're shooting inside, always face the window. If the lighting is too bright, try a sheer white curtain to mask some of it. If you want to turn your home into the perfect studio, a few of my friends in the business recommended http://www.cowboystudio.com for lighting, which I loved.

SHOOTING:

When filming on your phone, always turn it horizontally so the video file size can fill larger screens. If you only want to use the video for social media, vertical is perfect. Keep the bloopers, they are always hilarious. If you can, memorize your talking points or have them at eye level while you're shooting to help you stay on topic. Decide where you want to keep your eyes, to camera or just off, and be consistent. There's nothing weirder than creepy eyes that dart everywhere.

VIDEO EDITING:

I always use iMovie, but that is just because I know it really well. If you're just getting started, you might want to try Adobe Premiere. I have tons of friends who use that, and I am thinking I'll transition soon. Remember to get creative, adding in images and jump cuts. It keeps it fun and interesting. If you notice yourself rambling or saying "like" too much, cut away! Some YouTubers love long videos, but I personally prefer them around three minutes. If you want to download a video from YouTube and insert it in your video, try Video Grabby. Just make sure you have legal rights to it or are safe under the Fair Use law. I would explain more, but I'm not a copyright expert, and I promised a non-boring book.

When you post new content, always remember to promote and #share on all platforms. Ask fans to like, share, comment and subscribe. It's weird, but people really will do what you say.

Whatever platform you choose, make sure you build connectivity to your people and talk to them like they are your best friends. Know your voice in media, and stick to it. Being the first on a new platform is always the best way to grow the biggest. If you see a bunch of big social media influencers or celebs posting about a new platform, there's a good chance it's the next big thing. Try it out and see what you think. Oh, and always have a sales funnel on your site to capture email addresses.

Credit: Britt Barrett

DRIVE YOUR FAN BASE TO YOUR PLATFORM

Growing a platform comes down to two things: 1) your owned platform (your website or your blog) and 2) your promotional platforms (social media accounts). It's easier to grow your following on your owned platform (#1) if you're promoting it on social media channels (#2). Sure, Google does wonders to help people find your website when searching your keywords, but social media platforms are easier to stand out on because there's less content than the entire internet. That's why you should use "#2" to drive traffic to "#1."

Driving fan traffic to your platform works like this: let's say I have a product line (which I am in the process of developing right now, by the way) that sells in Barney's. First of all, that would be beyond FAB! They already have a high-end clientele, so I would monetize on the natural foot traffic to generate sales. We would all be very happy. But, what if they decided to stop promoting/supporting me? Or, what if they went out of business? That would suck. Suddenly, my fans have no idea where to buy my fabulous collection! Now, if I've done well (which I better have) with branding and engaging my fans/consumers outside the store and on my own platform ("#1"), I can continue selling to them online and/or let them know that I am moving to Neiman Marcus. Failing to do so would result in losing hundreds of thousands of dollars, from potential customers who can't find my product. If you lose the base you've worked so hard to build, you're screwed. Make sense? You don't want to be the loser who didn't have emails for your 5 million fans on Vine before they plugged the plug. You need to be ahead of the curve.

CHAPTER 6

GET #RELEVANT: Grow Your Fan Base

Fans get tired of the people who just want to look hot and make everything about them. Your fans want to connect with you. They need to know who you are and what you care about. Having fans is like having best friends. They like people who are like them. It all comes down to authenticity. I can't stand fake, and neither can you. I mean, one would assume.

Credit: Alphie Chikwashi

Just do us all a favor and don't let the industry get to your head. Sure, you may reach success and have a glamorous life, but it's never worth the emptiness, if you can't be who you really are. Don't take one fan, comment, like, heart, or conversation for granted. Yes, you'll have people who try to use you, stalk you, etc. You might even have a second when you believe your own press. Just make sure it's the shortest second of your life. Fame will change your "normal." If you can SLAY THE FAME GAME, your brand will be in demand, but if your new routine becomes such the norm that you forget how the rest of the world lives, you'll get out of touch real quick. That's not good for your heart or for connecting with fans. Never get so comfortable with success or press that you forget how to relate, be human, or keep your head on Earth.

HOW TO START

My guess is that you're already on social media. I mean, that is the obvious assumption after the last chapter. But, just in case you aren't, or are but don't have your branding on fleek, I'm going to take you through, step by step ...

REGISTER YOUR @HANDLE:

When creating your handle, make sure it fits your brand. Hopefully, you thought of a fabulous handle when creating your platform. Whatever you choose, make it memorable and use the same handle on every platform. You have to keep it consistent. You want to help people properly social stalk you.

USE A KILLER PROFILE PIC:

This is your first impression. It's important that you use an image so beautiful and compelling that people have to check you out and follow you. Imagine if someone accidentally stumbles on your profile when searching for another friend, you want your picture to grab them. Just keep it classy. I love a stunning headshot or something that looks like a gorgeous photo shoot.

PROFILE DESCRIPTION ON FLEEK:

This is where people decide if they like you or not. I know it sounds harsh, but you have about 150 characters to convince complete strangers to love you. Take your time, tell them what you do, give them a sneak peek of your personality, and include updated contact information. Make it easy to collaborate.

GROW IT, QUEEN!

The first thing everyone wants to know after they create an account is how to grow. I get it, the struggle is real. It's a popularity game, and everyone wants to feel popular. The key is engagement. Content matters, but if you aren't actively liking, commenting, engaging, and following, no one will find you.

POST GREAT CONTENT:

I know it seems obvious, but a lot of people just don't post good content. When studying people's liking habits, it's clear we all appreciate the images people worked for. Fabulous backgrounds, gorgeous outfits, perfect lighting, etc. Look, I realize this isn't great news for the girl who wants the easy fix, but it's true. People appreciate beauty, so make sure you're keeping your images beautiful and your feed consistent. Oh, and NEVER post practically the same shot fifteen times, even if it was gorgeous ... that's just weird. Fans love tips and tutorials, so try that and see how they respond.

Oh, and for some reason, statistics show that the color blue gets more engagement than others. I know it's random, but the research is there. So why not give it a try?

Use personal captions and appropriate hashtags. I use a couple hashtags in the caption, then comment right below with about ten or fifteen more. If you talk about fashion, don't share a weird photo of golf balls. I have no clue why or how that popped in my head, but it did. Just go with it, or more accurately, don't go with it, and certainly don't post it.

Credit: Britt Barrett

ENGAGE: As I mentioned a second ago, you won't grow if you don't engage with people. It is called "social" media for a reason, people! Don't be afraid to make the first move. The best strategy for this is to like and/or comment on three photos, then follow. This will provide enough of the stalk to get their attention, without creeping them out. Target celebs and influencers with similar brands, so you can engage with followers most likely to like you. Just make sure you have built up at least thirty images on your feed, before engaging with anyone. Most people won't follow you if you don't have any content yet. You can also troll (yes, I said "troll") hashtags that match your content so you can connect with people of similar interests.

FEATURE YOUR FANS:

People don't think enough about the ways they can make their fans happy. Why not give them a shout-out on your platform? Give them the love and support that they always give you. Can you imagine how much it would mean to them? Show them that you value them. You never know what a difference it could make in their life. Even just liking or commenting on their posts might mean a lot to them. I can't tell you how many times my followers have sent me messages saying they can't believe I've taken the time to respond. What they don't realize is that I read every note and they all mean the world to me.

PREZIES & GIVEAWAYS:

Credit: *Adam Kay*

Another fabulous way to grow your community is through giveaways. "*I wouldn't want a little social media surprise*," said no one ever! Collaborate with big influencers and you'll really grow! It doesn't matter what you do, just do something! Rafflecopter works well on websites and blogs, if you want to go that route. It's always great to be growing your list, so if they're sending you their email address and/or shipping address, you can always stay connected with them. The gifts don't have to be expensive, just creative: roses, a blow-out voucher, products, etc.

GET VERIFIED:

If you really want to stand out on social media, verification will do it. That little blue check mark will do wonders to stand out in comments and on your profile. But, how do you get it? Each platform is different. Facebook and Twitter are easy but Instagram is a little harder. I recommend using the service: www.starglamenterprise.com.

BE THE FIRST:

As I mentioned before, it's about being the first on a new platform. All my friends who have grown the biggest will always tell you that. Pay attention to new platforms on the market, and try them out. If you get traction, you just might luck out and be the next massive influencer! Also, don't be shy about contacting the founders of the latest app to collaborate. Worst case scenario they say no, but respect your hustle.

STAY CONSISTENT:

You want to create consistent content on your platforms. Videos should go up once a week, with images up daily. To protect your need for rest, you could do what I do: give yourself some lead time with content so you can look ugly a few days a week (you could never *really* look ugly) while posting old content. That will **SAVE** you on a demanding day, when you don't have time or energy for a glam day complete with a photo shoot.

Credit:
Britt
Barrett

I got caught doing that once, from the comfort of my home, in my PJs. A friend saw a photo pop up of me "at the Grove", and immediately texted to say she too was there. Oops! I had to quickly out myself that the photo was a month old. Of course she understood. It takes a lot of energy to get a brand moving. You don't want to ghost your fans on social too long, or you could lose them. Creating consistent content and engaging your fans will help you grow. If you find something that works, keep at it.

One thing that might help you post frequently (but no more than two to three times daily) is a scheduling tool. Try Hootsuite or Planoly. You can design everything, then post during your most engaging times.

Whatever the content strategy, make sure you are on the right platform and talking only about things that support your messaging. For example, let's say you were me,

GOING VIRAL

owning the fame game brand. First of all, congrats, it's really amazing! Haha! Of course, I was gonna throw that in ... sorry, I couldn't resist. Anyway, your topics need to all be aligned with the strategy to "SLAY THE FAME GAME." I wouldn't all of the sudden talk about cats or random furniture. That would be weird. Even if it would help me go viral. It doesn't make any sense. It also doesn't make sense to post content that isn't currently trending. If you haven't quite mastered the whole "be the story" thing, you need to learn to ride the waves of trending stories. More on this in the next chapter.

To ride media waves, you need to cover trending stories that are going viral. Let's say it is about a celeb getting out of rehab. I could post a video encouraging them on taking that step towards their future, with some advice to manage stress in the industry. See how we covered the trend but didn't change my brand messaging? Always think of ways to cover a trending story, but bring it back to your messaging ... giving tips, making jokes, blah, blah, blah.

Same if you decided to make a brand all about feeling great about your body. Ride trending stories about fitness, then remind your audience to love themselves where they are ... today! Not after they lose or gain some lbs.

CHAPTER 7 *"YOU'RE WELCOME!"*
... BE THE EXPERT

To get interviewed on morning shows like KTLA, the Today Show, and by the GORGEOUS Kelly Ripa, you need to be an expert able to help people by sharing tips. Whether you're a model, sharing Emmy's trends, or an author sharing tips to "SLAY THE FAME GAME," you need to make sure your content is educational and helpful. To be invited on shows like that, you need to know how to brag about your abilities in a classy way.

Keep your head in the game and be confident enough to pitch yourself when the opportunity pops up.

Last night, I showed up at an event I was halfway invited to. Meaning, I didn't receive the invite (which hurt the top half of my ego) so I was attending as a plus one. It wouldn't have been that painful to the bottom half of my ego, except for the fact that it was a last-minute invite, so I wasn't dressed up enough. We arrived when it was ending, so security on one side of the building didn't want to let us in. Of course, all my friends are very Hollywood, which means they don't take no for an answer. So, we walked past that security guard to the other entrance. But, with the event wrapping up, it was a paparazzi frenzy with celebs rushing from the venue to their SUVs every few minutes. Since I wasn't sure we would get in, I hung back in the side alley, as our friend called the owner to get us in. The last thing I needed was a TMZ video of a bouncer giving me the hand. Eww, career killer. I looked to my left, and there was a friendly crackhead having an—ahem —"experience" with whatever he was on. All I could think was, "*Umm, am I really missing couch time with my Chihuahuas, to wait outside at a party I don't really want to go to*??" Needless to say, I ended up ordering an Uber and telling our friend we would catch him later. Of course, this whole experience had me going home feeling like an alleyway loser with no invite. But, I stopped to grab a late-night bite and ended up meeting a producer who, when she heard my life's story, wanted to interview me on her show! Look, I realize this story is full of first world, Hollywood problems. But, the point is, if I were to let the night's earlier ego blows keep me down, I wouldn't be willing to throw on that smile and slay my humble brag.

You have to stay positive, no matter what comes up. Never take the industry too seriously. Some people will treat you like a star, some will mistake you for the bathroom attendant and ask you for a paper towel. Never think of yourself or anyone else as less or better than the next person. Just focus on educating yourself to be an expert in the areas you're most passionate about, and SLAY.

Don't stop when you're starting to trend. Keep pushing. Keep going to those meetings and never get a head too big to audition. Make it a priority, even when it's easier to be lazy. I remember going to see my family in Georgia, but changing my flight to return a little earlier, on the way back, so I could make it to an event. To get ready for it, I changed in the tiny airplane bathroom. It wasn't very graceful. I was all up in my own stuff, hitting my head on the door while trying to hook my heels, but I pushed through the annoyance to make it work. Oh, and don't waste your faux eyelashes on a party with no agenda. Make a goal for the event and plan to meet a few people to practice your pitch on.

Credit: Britt Barrett

KNOW YOUR TOPIC

I know it might shock you, but the first step to being an expert is actually knowing what you're talking about (notice the sarcasm). Depending on your content strategy and brand, your topic should open the conversation for your passion. Don't be an expert in travel if your passion is modeling. Focus all your attention on what you love, and expand on that.

My brand is all about encouraging ladies to live fabulous lives. And, since I have lived it and am writing the book on entertainment, I am uniquely qualified as an expert in the entertainment industry. Specifically, breaking into the business and not letting it break you. That helps anyone from a twelve-year-old with a big social media following to a thirty-year-old whose dream is to act on a hit TV show. This industry can be hard on the heart, so I can share tips from years of self help books, running a support group, and overcoming some crap myself. I can also talk about social media, beauty, fashion, hater trolls ... pretty much anything that fits the fame game.

What is your brand? What can you share that will help others live better lives? Show producers seek guests and topics that will engage and entertain their audience. Because, like you, they are in the content curation business, with platforms that need engaged fans, so they can sell ads to brands.

MAKE IT RELEVANT

Being informed about your topic is great. Having that be a topic that brings value to its audience is even better. But, if it isn't a trending conversation, you won't get very far with it in mainstream media. That means, you need to research what trends in press, so you can create current responses in media. It's like riding a wave in the ocean. If it already has momentum, you can get swept right up into it with little effort ... unless you're me on a surfboard, in which case, you would just go right under water!

A perfect example of riding the wave is my friend Roger Tsai. He is a talented, Beverly Hills plastic surgeon, who knows how to grow his practice. Roger is strategic about getting on shows and being a part of any conversation. This gets his name in press. One way he does this is by paying attention to big celebrity stories regarding plastic surgery. Every time a story comes out about whether a celeb has gone under the knife, Roger is ready to ride the media wave by commenting publicly on the story. For example, let's say People Magazine is talking about whether or not Kylie Jenner got lip injections (hmmm, do we really not know?). Roger could contact the "tips" email address and let them know that he is available to comment. If asked, he can type up comments so the reporter can easily copy/paste them into their article, if they would like.

The key is to stay relevant and make it fast and easy. Reporters and journalists are incredibly busy. If you want to stay on their good side, you need to be thorough and responsive. For example, you could send something like this:

New Message

To: Fabulous Blogger or Journalist

Subject: Alleged Lip Injections/Quote by Plastic Surgeon

Hi ___Name of reporter on story_,

I saw your fabulous article on People.com on _____'s lips. As a board certified plastic surgeon at _Company_, I would love to share my professional opinion on whether she had lip injections, below:

Name: Roger Tsai, board certified plastic surgeon at Inject Me
Comment: While I did not treat Kylie, it certainly appears that ...

Feel free to copy/paste or reply with any questions, as you see fit.

S E N D

SIT ON PANELS

Another great way to solidify your brand as a topic expert is to sit on panels and volunteer as a keynote speaker or moderator. Maybe you go to Beautycon and discuss makeup, maybe you host a monthly photo shoot like mine in Hollywood, to help people slay the fame game and pursue their dreams. There are so many ways to build the perception and recognition as an expert, so research the opportunities, pitch yourself and follow up until you get an answer. Just don't be a pest. Nobody likes that! More on pitching in Chapter eight.

One great organization I have spoken to about collaborating with is I Am That Girl. They are all about female empowerment, so maybe you connect with your local chapter to see if you can get involved and help them with a women's event where you can speak. If it's your first time speaking, make sure you've practiced a lot, and have your talking points on hand. I highly recommend bringing in a friend or videographer to capture the talk, so you can add it to your sizzle.

WHAT ARE YOUR TOP 10?

A great way to encourage people to talk about you as an expert is to provide a sample blog post or downloadable document that shares your top 10 tips to _____. For my brand, sharing my "Top 10 Tips to SLAY THE FAME GAME" makes a lot of sense. This is a great way to share some helpful advice and get your name out in media. Plus, if you have a link on your website or platform to download the document after sharing your email, you can grow your list and use it to share updates on speaking engagements, events, and new content.

PERCEPTION IS EVERYTHING

Right now, it is all about building your reputation as an expert. Sure, you might not *feel* like an expert. In fact, you may feel more like a moron or a fraud. Don't worry, we ALL feel like that sometimes! I have been working in this industry for eight years, but I still feel like a loser sometimes. That's why I am writing this book. One of the more talented people I know, a PhD and incredibly smart guy had his own doubts when he started writing his book. He was nervous that his peers would think he thought way too much of himself or that they would hate on him. The reality is, they might, but who cares? When you have something important to say, you should say it! Especially if it will truly help someone. Sure, someone could have taught the exact same thing before you, but they don't have your perspective or your voice. Who knows, you may be the only person who can get through to someone.

It's easy to think, "Umm, fashion is not curing cancer, it's not that important." But can you imagine the impact it might have on someone who might be in an unhealthy relationship and doesn't feel beautiful or lovable? Maybe your words inspire her to feel fabulous and beautiful, or help her feel more confident. She might even overcome some insecurities and realize she deserves more than the relationship she's in. You never know how you might help someone, so don't doubt yourself. Have confidence and use your social platforms to promote your work. Sure, in the beginning, you might need to use a little creative writing (like an endorsement from your mom ... signed off with her maiden name) to sound respected in the community. But, the more people give you a shot, the more chances you have to build your resume and your confidence.

FAKE EYELASHES ARE AS FAUX AS I GET

I know it can feel a little scary to fake it 'til you make it. Trust me, I get it. In fact, before I go one step—or, more accurately, one word further—I need to do that whole, confessional stuff. You see, I know that perception is everything, and bragging about your brand is necessary, but I personally get super uncomfortable doing it! I also have no poker face. The good news for you is that if you happen to know how to brag a little bit, you're in good company. This is the industry where people say they are "filmmakers" when they've never even read a full script, let alone produced or made one. So, don't feel bad as you build a brand that looks bigger than you really are. Before this book, you may have never heard of me before. Yet, if you Google my name, you may see stuff or people you recognize. I wouldn't have even been invited to half of those events, let alone be the name host of them, if I hadn't built a brand bigger than me. I felt like a TOTAL fraud (still do sometimes), but it is actually much more normal than you realize. So, don't stress about it!

P.S. Random rant: So many people in this industry "stretch" the truth. They say things like, "*Oh my gosh! Of course I know him!*" They don't. Or, "*Yes, I would love to grab coffee and catch up!*" They don't. My favorite is the filmmaker who is "*working on some really cool projects, but just can't talk about them yet.*" They aren't. But, I don't blame them. I mean, I judge them but I don't blame them. If they can act like they are BFF with Quentin Tarantino, you can build a brand prepared for the massive success you are about to have. When laying the foundation for a skyscraper, you don't design a duplex when your dream includes a 77th floor penthouse. Think big.

Don't wait until you feel like a true expert before you start. It takes a little good ole bravery, but put yourself out there! My man has his master's studies from Oxford and Pepperdine. He has launched over two hundred movies, companies, and TV shows, but he still gets nervous when putting himself out there. Don't worry about what people are going to think. Start doing, succeeding, failing, and trying. When I go a few months without a speaking engagement, I get nervous and think I'll have nothing to say. Then, I go on stage and remember that I'm Southern and could talk to a fruit fly. Don't wait until you feel perfect. Be you, flaws and all! You can always do a little extra research in your field; in fact, I recommend it. The more educated you are, the more your topic will come to life.

Don't make the mistake of not understanding this crazy game called PR. Nerds will tell you it stands for "public relations," which is technically true but it is all about "personal relationships." You see, most people won't lift a finger in this town if it doesn't benefit them. Sorry to come down on your Cinderella fairytale like a bulldozer, but it's true. That's why you need to be the talent that people can't say no to. Focus on being the first to bring value and be fabulous. People will love you and want to introduce you to all the producers, directors, agents, managers, and publicists they can think of.

People want to make themselves look good. So, if you're kind, talented, humble, down to earth, helpful, grateful, and fun, they know a referral will make them look good. Productions need great talent as much as you need great jobs. This isn't the land of mediocrity, so you need to stand out.

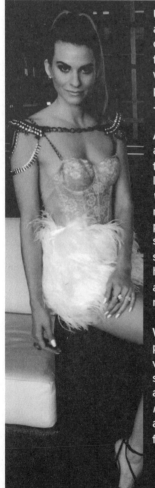

Unfortunately, not all talent is considered equal. I had a girl work with me for about six months, but she could not figure out my world. I would fight dramatic frustration when she would schedule meetings ... with no location. Or, would set up calls and NEVER provide or request a contact number!! Deep breaths ... Namaslay, namaslay, namaslay.

Anyway, her last night with me was the red carpet for a film premiere. She kept freezing up because it was the biggest red carpet she had ever done. I was literally saying, between a frozen smile, "*VWalk, vwalk, vwalk*!" That's how it sounds when you aren't moving your lips, by the way. Whatever. It was painful. I was in a line trying to walk in my gown, but she was FROZEN in front of me. Fans would take selfies with me—even though there's a chance they had zero clue who I was—but she would just awkwardly stand there photobombing them all. I remember just praying her brain would turn back on.

We were just about to (barely) survive the photographers so I could do interviews with the videographers at the end of the line. This is where she is supposed to walk up to each interviewer and ask, "*Would you like to discuss fashion trends with model and author Rachel McCord?*" But, she froze again! Right there, photobombing all my shots in front of about fifteen photographers.

It was BEYOND painful. I literally had to walk around her to finish the photo line. Then, in front of everyone, I had to remind her to go talk to each of the interviewers. Did she walk up gracefully, start a conversation and inquire about their interest in interviewing me? Oh no, honey, she looked from left to right, in complete terror, then fanning her arms out, as if she was offering a plate of shrimp, yelled (yes, I said yelled) out to everyone from E! News to TMZ, "*Anyone wanna talk to Rachel?*" I melted. I'm talking Cruella de Vil style (all internally, of course).

In reality, I just walked off the carpet ... as fast as humanly possible.

Credit: Britt Barrett

GET YOUR HEAD IN THE FAME GAME

Keep in mind that fame is not the most important thing you slay in life. My hope for you, obvi, is that you do tons of good in the world. It's important that you give back and keep things in perspective. You have to remember that you're choosing a rollercoaster career with many ups and downs. Don't start pitching yourself and then believing all your press. You're special because you slay the fame game. You're special because you're human. Which means that everyone else is special too. Keep good people around you. Don't be a climber or a user. Be as nice to your valet guy as you are to your dream CAA agent. Focus on keeping a level head and stay logical.

Most people don't talk about the feelings that pop up when they hit insane success in a short period of time. They usually hold it inside, thinking no one gets it. Authenticity isn't just good for content. It is great for relationships. And, good, healthy relationships are what staying unbroken in this industry is all about. You've already got me! I'll be the first person to tell you how weird all this is. In fact, I just started "*The Rachel McCord Show*" to talk about that. But, as much as I need a community of normal, awesome people to be real with ... you do too! Don't try and make this industry normal; you stay normal.

Keep your boundaries in check. I'm a swimsuit model. I'm constantly photographed with little clothes on. But, I have my limits too. I ran out of fashion tape a few weeks ago, and, on a red carpet, I not only had a "nip slip," I had a whole nip appearance. The whole freaking thing was out for the world to see! Fortunately, the press photog didn't capture it. Only the house photographer did. When asked by the event publicist, a close friend of mine, if I wanted her to push it to press, I said no. These things may happen accidentally, but 200 million impressions are not worth your self-respect. If you don't feel comfortable or it doesn't fit your brand, it is never worth the cost to trend for one day.

Pitching yourself is weird because it is us putting ourselves out there. Being vulnerable. But, you have to do it, if you dream of success in this industry. I was snubbed on a red carpet and it sucked. In fact, I was so snubbed, I had a photographer walk off the carpet when I arrived because he didn't know who I was. I felt like the loser who got passed over at the lunch room. But, I kept smiling and I moved on. I didn't stop pitching myself. I just kept going. That same week, I had three, full Daily Mail spreads, with one calling me a "Rising Star." If I had turned the red carpet snub into a panic concern of falling into obscurity like Brandi Glanville's late career, I might not have kept going for it. The Hollywood struggle is real, but you have got to keep getting back up and going for your dream!

MAKE HEADLINES

To SLAY THE FAME GAME, you need to create your own grassroots marketing campaign. The key is to start slowly start creeping into everything. First, start attending events, then show up at hotspots, network with publicists, do favors, intern for legit people in the business. Basically, look at it like full time photobombing. Not really ... but kind of. To get your name out there, you need to build friendships with everyone. Be kind, help out, bring value, etc. If you can't make celeb friends, just leave venues at the same time and stand awkwardly close. Maybe grab their arm (you could act like you're falling) but laugh hard and smile (unless you have the same head vein that I do ... in which case, smize) for the paparazzi. I'm obviously joking. But, you get the point. Be everywhere. Meet everyone. Be kind. Never burn a bridge. Have fun. Stay connected with family. If you do all that, you're well on your way. Just look at it as Strategic Trending, Duh. Or, STD for short. Oh, my gosh. I think I need a nap right now. <insert face palm here>

Wanna know someone who did all of the above and succeeded? My good friend, Clinton, an amazingly talented photographer told me what Kim Kardashian would do to get on the map, back in the Paris Hilton days. Legally, I think this is hearsay, which basically means I have to say "allegedly." So, allegedly, Kim would tell him when she was showing up at a hotspot with Paris Hilton, back in ancient years, and pay him $50 to take her photo and yell her name in front of other paparazzi. She even, allegedly, went on a date with Nick Lachey, and surprisingly enough, even though they weren't followed into the dark movie theatre, there was a crowd of photographers waiting for them as they left. She dodged questions about their "relationship" for weeks after. Done and done.

GET AN "ASSISTANT"

Before you can get in press, you need to have "someone" to pitch you. Now, I realize that you probably don't have a lot of revenue coming in from your dream job. It takes time to build that, but don't sweat. There are some tricks (most people use) that will keep you from looking like a loser while pitching yourself.

The truth is, you have two options. Each starts with you getting a new email for your assistant. Before I had permanent p e o p l e , I h a d : *Assist.Rachel@themccordlist.com*. That way, as people popped in to help me for a few weeks or months, I wasn't changing their name every week. It is up to you, but I highly recommend creating one.

When hiring someone, you have a few options: 1) hire someone to work a few hours every week, 2) do an internship program (just make sure it is legit), 3) use Fiverr to outsource work. You could also be your own "assistant" by emailing people "on behalf of" yourself. It makes it less awkward when securing your rate.

Credit: Hamid Moslehi

Either way you need that email address for your assistant or "assistant." Oh, and if it is you, pretending to be "them," make sure the first thing you do when you create a new email is to sign off with the "assistant's" name. There's nothing more awkward than signing off as yourself when you're trying pretend like you're someone else. Oops!

GLAM UP YOUR PITCH

People need to know how fabulous you are. I used to think I needed to wait until someone else told them. Then, Christine Peak, a fabulous publicist with Peake PR Group taught me that *"We need to tell the world, Darling!"*. She wasn't joking. In this business, people want you to get to the point ... FAST in a pitch! You need to approach this like the legit business it is. You need to produce marketing materials to encourage people to interview you.

Media Kit - You need a media kit to share in every pitch, until you have slayed so much that everyone knows. The first page should include a GORGEOUS headshot and your bio. Page two should include your social media reach (if it's impressive) along with a screenshot from your best posts and a blurb on the type of content you post. The remaining pages, excluding the last, should be press clippings from stories you were covered in. If you don't have any, go on Fiverr and pay about ten bloggers to write compelling stories about you. Which means, you write a compelling story and send it to them to post. The final page is the contact information for your assistant.

Create a sizzle reel. This should tell the story of who you are, what talent(s) you have and what your mission is. The story of mine is guided along by one in-depth interview I was covered in. Whatever you do, make sure it's professional, captures your personality and connects you to the audience.

Order some business cards. You need to give them out when you attend events and meet new people. You don't want to take away from your celeb brand, so just make sure they are classy and include your agent or assistant's contact information. I LOVE Moo for business card orders. You can be cheap, but you'll probably hate the first ones and end up going with Moo in the end.

GET YOUR PLAN TOGETHER

<u>Here are some basics to remember before pitching:</u>

1. Know your story
2. Know the trending stories
3. Know your end goal
4. Prepare for the call to action

For me, with my upcoming press tour, I know that **my story** is about my passion to help people break into entertainment without it breaking them (like it has done me a few times). The **trending stories** that fit are all about social media and the impact it has on their self-confidence and the obsession with perfectionism. My **end goal** is to remind audiences of the importance of loving themselves, staying positive, being real and not taking all this too seriously. The **call to action** is to check out my book, attend my events in Hollywood, and sign up for the email list on my blog, The McCord List.

If you haven't already, take a minute to iron out the above before pitching. (Oh my gosh, what is this? 1904? That saying is so old school!)

Publicists use a list called Cision, which shares the emails for every press and media outlet. There is also Celebrity Intelligence to reach every celeb's team. You want access to Cision and a feature on Celebrity Intelligence. This particular section is all about Cision, and your personal list. Most publicists are not going to share an export of their Cision list for no reason, but, if you happen to know someone fabulous, you just might luck out. If not, maybe after you make friends with one, you -can offer them a little cash for some contacts. You can also pull them one by one by clicking on the contact link for any outlet you want to pitch. Cision is great because you can search keywords and download the most recent contact for media who covers the topic.

If you don't know how to get your hands on that list, it's okay! There are other solutions to getting you that press. You can build your own list. I know it sounds like a lot. That's because it is. But, it will be well worth it if you build that list through true relationship, versus data dump.

Follow these steps below for the best way to create your list:

1. Create a spreadsheet. I prefer Google Sheets, because it is saved online through your Google Drive, so you can access it anywhere, anytime.

2. Use the header row (1) to describe each column. I use the following headers for each column:
   - First name
   - Last name
   - Email address
   - Instagram URL
   - Total following
   - Blog site
   - Total following
   - Notes
   - Worked with in the past? Yes/No

3. Everything above is pretty self-explanatory, except columns G and H. You can pull the website numbers from SimilarWeb.com. For notes, I use this as a note to jog my memory about who they are and what they write about

4. Writers want to feel acknowledged for their hard work. Think about it, they spend every day promoting and encouraging other people. It is important they be acknowledged for their work. So, when you find them during channel mapping, be sure to make a note to help you remember them for later.

To build your list, you can use social media and Google searches. Just start with your ideal press contact and start looking for similar account recommendations. Instagram is the easiest platform for this, but feel free to use whichever platform(s) you like. Most content creators share their email address in their profiles or the contact page of their website.

START PITCHING

When people in this industry aren't working they drive themselves (and sometimes me) crazy! The slow times in your career are meant to be spent working on the business of you. This is the best time to update your pitch materials, pitch yourself, etc. Don't be lazy or too busy with busy-ness that you don't work on the business of you.

This is the perfect time to earn some media for yourself. However, it's shocking how many people send awful pitches. It's almost like they are so focused on what they want, they forget what it means to earn media. Earned media is when you truly *earn* coverage. This is different than posting on owned channels (like your own blog or social media) or doing some media buys (also referred to as "paid), where you pay money to say what you want for advertising.

Credit: Britt Barrett

To earn the media, you need to share content that is EASY! Content creators are super busy! They need easy pitches that are interesting and engaging. That means you need to send them the article practically written ... in their voice.

Always include images, but make sure you own them. They could get sued for that Google image you scraped off the web.

Begin by mentioning a recent article and sharing a compliment on their site. This is where your list notes come in. **My favorite way to reach out is like this:**

1. Greeting/compliment.

2. Share why you're requesting the coverage (I work with __your name____, and we would be honored if you would cover __her new shoot___ because ...). Make sure whatever reason you share is a currently trending story. Otherwise, you're thinking about their need to ride the viral wave, like we discussed with your content.

3. Sign off with a big thank you, and, if you can, some gift or offer, if they choose to share it for you.

4. Enclose the sample blog post below, or go ahead and attach it as a separate document and attach images.

Always remember to follow up. They are VERY busy and VERY overwhelmed with pitches. Be kind ALWAYS! They don't owe you anything ... ever! If they share your story, it is out of kindness/interest. Keep working on your email template until you hit gold that works with numerous outlets, then use it all the time ... and send it to me. =)

If they end up posting, always say thank you and follow through on whatever they offered you. Star them in your spreadsheet and stay connected. Follow and engage with them on social media, share their stories (not just the ones about you), and build a friendship. You don't need 1,000 outlets, you only really need about twenty to fifty in your pocket.

Credit: Leo Deveney

Here are some extra tips on pitching:

- Know the press outlet
- Dedicate a few hours every day to pitch
- Pull up those old business cards to see which media connections you already have
- Be passionate but not too long-winded
- Be confident and show your successes
- Create a personal connection
- Keep it short and easy to read with lots of white space
- Never lie ... duh
- Save sample blog posts as PDFs. Don't send in a weird, Word format
- NO TYPOS! I meannnnn, need I say more?
- Make sure the subject could easily be a story headline
- Don't use hyperlinks. Type out the links you plan to use
- Get to the point quickly: I'd like share a story on..."
- If you meet in person, pay the bill. OBVIOUSLY. Or offer to bring them coffee or lunch if you meet at their office
- 50-60 people is the magic number to get a yes on cold pitches
- It's a numbers game. Don't sweat rejection
- Stay on top of your emails
- Follow up is most important
- Constantly check industry sites like HARO, for reporters seeking quotes and help with stories
- Send thank you within 24 hours even if they don't publish you
- Check in 2 months after your initial pitch, then after another 3 - 4 months. Continue to follow up every 6 months, just to stay connected. But keep follow up short

Events + Red Carpets

If you plan to walk the red carpet (which you should), you need to find someone to play publicist to pitch you for the night. Trust me when I tell you, it sucks to show up at a red carpet event without a handler.

You need someone to take charge, walk you where you are supposed to go (even if they have no clue) and escort you down the line with your slate (basically a piece of paper with your name printed bolded and large —which you probably just printed for yourself in your red carpet dress at the Kinkos one mile away). This is them literally pitching you to press.

Oh, and make sure you discuss the plan ahead of time. If they aren't a full-time publicist and haven't done this before, ask them to pay attention to what other *real* publicists do, once you get there.

Part of the planning process should be having a solid interview pitch for the end of the carpet line. Unless you want to enjoy the Cruella de Vil moment I mentioned earlier!

Since you might not be on the talent list, you need them to be a little Olivia Pope! The event publicist (aka the person guarding the red carpet) may say, "Who is that?" "Are they on the talent list?" (aka tip sheet, which is a piece of paper with celebrities' names and headshots). Whatever they ask, the real answer is probably "no." But tonight it's, "Duh, yes!" Don't let them see weakness or insecurity. You need your "publicist" ready to say yes and help you get in front of those cameras. They, on your behalf, need to be kind, but firm. He/she needs to say: "My 'client' (aka the girl who just hired me off Craigslist) is walking this carpet. It's happening. Period." Yass, Queen! If you find someone like that, send them my way!

Credit: Britt Barrett

Oh, and the photographers and videographers may have no clue who you are. They didn't know who I was for the longest time. Some still don't. Don't feel bad. That's what your faux publicist is for. They are there to sell you.

Don't feel bad if they don't get any takers on interviews during the first couple of pitches. In fact, you shouldn't even be within earshot to know if they said no. Just move slowly enough behind them that you "have NO idea what they are doing." Don't stand there, awkwardly staring, like, "*WELL, don't you want to interview me*?!" That would be terrible, and I would feel guilty by association.

When you get your interview, be sure to compliment the host. No one ever does that and they should! Also, have your "publicist" grab their card at the end for follow up. For more tips on interviewing, check out Chapter nine.

I know this all can sound like a lot of stress, don't worry, it is. It's terrifying, emotionally draining, and exhausting. But, it's also amazing and fun! Just remember to breathe.

YOU WON'T ALWAYS GET IN PRESS

You should know, even if you attend the right event and perfectly slay your style, you won't always get the press. I know, it's annoying! There could be a million reasons. But it happens to the best of us. So, before you change your name to Tara Reid 2.0 and have a memorial service for your career, take a breath and shake it off. There's always tomorrow. Besides, I completely understand the feeling, so you aren't alone. I know how much it sucks to be rejected.

I recently splurged on a $20 bodysuit from Forever 21 for a red carpet premiere. Let's just say I was feelin' myself. I had on new shoes and two hours of my makeup on my face (I love leisure makeup application in front of my favorite shows).

All ready to go, I did my whole, runway walk to the Uber. It was just arriving! A fresh, 2011 Toyota Camry--. Wait, what? Ummm, okay … That is, umm, a look. Okay. I apparently ordered the wrong tier. But, no stress. No one is going to see this, I reasoned. I just needed to take a deep breath and have this nice driver open the door from the inside … you know, because the outside handle was broken. It's all good. I grew up in trailer parks, I can survive this.

The driver was so nice, so I kinda felt bad for mentally dissing his car. So sorry, my favorite new driver! Soon, we rolled up on Hollywood Boulevard, and hopped out ... IN FRONT OF THE NIKE STORE! Ahem, excuse me? Surely, this is not the destination? Especially since Hollywood Boulevard is known for all the comic characters who hang out. I was starting to look like a faux cat woman in a bodysuit, looking for tips for photos.

You can understand the urgency for my man to lead the charge and get me to a nice place that matched my outfit ... STAT! This could not have come soon enough.

Of course, Rick, trying to be a gentleman was allowing me to walk ahead. I spun around like a toddler, in those uncomfortable (yet, chic) new heels, grabbed his arm and pulled him in front of me. He was the only one among us who knew where to go, and I needed him to GET US THERE. We finally made it inside, past all the jaw drops we got as we walked past Wetzel Pretzel. P.S., I would have given my faux fur wrap to have a pepperoni pretzel right about then. However, that bodysuit was hugging me tighter than my first boyfriend ... so we all knew that was not an option.

Finally, we made it through the woods and over the hills to the red carpet. I did the line and had a fabulous time doing my positive affirmations: *"Oh yes, I'm killing this," "Werk, werk, werk, werk, werk."* What? I didn't say it was profound...

Unfortunately, here is where the story unravels ... The next morning, I did my daily devotional. Yassss! Then, I excitedly log in into my email to check all the Google Alerts on "Rachel McCord" from last night. Hmm, weird. No mention of me. Only some blog in Brazil talking about ABC's old show Castle (which my cousin by marriage named a character Rachel McCord after me on ... my greatest non-accomplishment yet!). Okay, no sweat, we got this. Enter: www.DailyMail.com. I did a fabulous job of not getting distracted by the random stories in the feed. Okay, I only got distracted by one or two. Okay, ten ... max. Just as I was beginning to think they snubbed the event, I see it roll up on my screen. Yay! My moment to shine, y'all! I scroll through all 14 pictures, and, it wasn't until I got to 13 that I realize it wasn't looking too good for me. Nope. No coverage. Umm, okay. Okay. Not exactly what I was hoping for or expecting but that's okay, I can be mature-- ARE YOU KIDDING ME?!?! Two hours of makeup, a bodysuit, uncomfortable heels, no pretzel!?! I could have stayed on my couch and done a little Netflix one-on-one.

The reason I'm sharing that embarrassing story is because we all have hits and misses in this industry. Don't take them seriously. I remember (not long ago ... at all), trying to elbow my way onto a red carpet. Now, I'm in press a lot. But I never take it for granted. Just keep patting yourself on the back for showing up. This industry has a way of making you feel like a loser (when you weren't invited to that fabulous event), insecure (when you walk past other gorgeous Queens in the business), and like a dork (when you pitch yourself). But that doesn't mean you should ever feel insecure. Be supportive of your work and others. Don't take this job too seriously. Oh, and if you want that pretzel ... you get it, girl!

CHAPTER 9
PERFECT IT: Interviews & Media Training

When I did my first on-camera interview, I was a hot mess. Just less of the hot, more of the mess. I was at SKYBAR at Mondrian, and it was with this really sweet interviewer before the Grammys. He was a little, umm, old ... so talking pop culture was a bit of a stretch for him. Of course, if he had read my book maybe it would have helped him develop his own brand a little better. He could have either dropped the suit or the Hollywood topics. The two didn't fit together. He was still super cute, though.

The funniest thing about our interview wasn't his suit, though. It was the fact that we were both a little lost. He was acting ancient and I was feeling insecure. At that stage in my career, I felt like someone could have blown a deep breath and knocked me over. I was insecure, rooted in nothing, and kind of lost with my brand. I felt like the girl no one should have let in. Of course, I would hide that crap as best I could, but deep down that's how I felt. There's a big difference in this business when you have a strong handle on what you're doing, where you're going, and why you're heading there. If you believe in something or someone bigger than yourself, you can re-center yourself and find your purpose. Of course, I had no clue what my purpose was, so I didn't have direction in interviews.

What I did have was crappy internal dialogue that, although was never spoken, definitely translates on screen. I don't know how but it does. It's almost like a question can come up and your insecure brain will tell you, "*This is an attack, I must defend myself!*" Meanwhile, snap to reality, the other person is like, *Umm, I was just asking who made your dress.*" Hi, confusion. He was just running through his list of questions. That's obviously just a silly example of how your brain can play tricks on you. But it is a good reminder of how important it is to get your head in the game before you put yourself out to millions of people with millions of opinions, excuses to be jealous, etc.

Of course, it was reasons like that interview that had me breathing panic and made me realize I had to write this book. I know the crap that comes up. I mean, this guy is asking who I wanted to win, while I'm wondering why I wore this ugly denim jacket, and all I could think was, "Win where?" His response, "For the Grammys. We are at a Grammys event, you know!" Oh crap. That's right. Earth to Rachel! Think of someone, QUICK. "Be-yonn-ce...?" Was she nominated? Was that a dumb statement? Who knows! All I could think was, I need to say a name of someone who is probably up for something. The rest of his questions were a blur, as were my responses, which were all followed by nervous laughs, because all I could think was, "Was Beyoncé nominated or not!?!??"

Credit: Hamid Moslehi

LEARN FROM MY MISTAKES AND SLAY

There are many lessons to learn from my interview, which, surprisingly enough, didn't go viral. Hmm, I wonder why! The first one is to make sure you know what trending topics are happening. ESPECIALLY if you happen to be at an event FOR one of those trending topics. Being politically correct is important, but so is being a little interesting, unique and funny. Which is basically code for: make sure you're in the know about where you are, why you're there, what your message is and then be yourself × 100. You have to be "ON," when you're on camera. Now is not the time to have the personality of a paper bag. It is your moment to be fun, likeable, opinionated, strong and beautiful. Tell your story. Stick with your personal talking points. You also want to keep in mind, if you're interviewed on a red carpet, that you have to stand out if you want your interview featured in the event segment. Which you do ... obviously. One thing to help with this is to organically plug the event and their sponsors. If you are an organic advertisement for the event, the publicist will likely pitch your piece to press and want it included in the brand roundup. Keep them happy because they decide what gets pitched to news outlets and what doesn't. Remember to post a big thank you on your social media and platform channels, mentioning the sponsors. That will almost guarantee an invite to the next event.

In the last chapter, you learned to pitch yourself to sound like the Queen you are. Now, you need to make sure you're captivating and entertaining during interviews. To do this, you need to be an interesting human. Don't just stare at the camera, romance it! The more bubbly, sweet fun and surprising you are, the better! Controversial also works if it fits your brand. Get people staring, feeling intrigued, shocked, entertained, etc. Mainly, keep them interested and wanting more. DON'T come across as a stuck up, entitled, spoiled little rich Queen with no layers. Which basically means, don't be that person EVER.

Hollywood and social fans love a good story. You should learn to tell yours effectively. That means you need to stay on topic with the message you want to convey. If you don't have a book, film, or TV show to promote, your goal should be to just make them fall in love with you. Be yourself and don't hold back. If you're nervous, tell them! Be down to earth. No one likes people who constantly brag about themselves. You need to find a way to communicate your story in a humble way (i.e. your humble brag).

Credit:
Britt Barrett

ENTERTAINMENT

SLAY THAT HUMBLE BRAG!

The strategy behind telling your story on and off camera relies on six basic points:

1. Know your backstory and talking points.
2. Understand what you have working for you.
3. Familiarize yourself with your strengths.
4. Keep the conversation fun and engaging.
5. Make sure it is helpful and relevant, bringing direct value to the audience.
6. Pay attention to what you're asked in each interview, and how the interviewer responds to your answers. Iterate and become better and better.

To pull all that together, on and off camera, when someone asks, "What do you do?", you need to know your "humble brag." The goal is to share your story while bringing value to the audience. To help you out, I'll share an example of mine. Don't judge me.

Here goes:

"I'm a model, author, entrepreneur, and talk show host. Being featured in Vogue and Daily Mail is a huge blessing, and I'm super grateful. But, to be honest, I'm most passionate about my speaking appearances and show. I'm honored to speak and use the "Rachel McCord Show: from trailer parks to red carpets," to share my crazy life and Hollywood experiences with at-risk teens, aspiring talent, creatives, and entrepreneurs. I love to remind them that no matter where they come from or what they've been through, they deserve a fabulous life. I use my book, "SLAY THE FAME GAME" and volunteer work to that."

Do you get it? It's a humble way of sharing everything I'm working on. Most people don't know how important it is to have a strong backstory ready to go when they start a public life. I remember first arriving in Hollywood and being completely stumped with people wanting to know where I came from and what my story was. In hindsight, it probably would have done me a whole lotta good (yes, I'm Southern) to wait a beat and figure that out. Fortunately, you, my love, will not need to make that mistake. I guess I had good instincts because when people asked, I would say my family was in the industry, and that I had two older (stunningly gorgeous) sisters. Needless to say, they went wild. Of course, even though I was making a pretty good choice by naturally connecting dots that I was aligned in the entertainment industry, I didn't really know what I was doing because I didn't even know what being a brand meant. Let alone that I *was* one.

Credit: Britt Barrett

I have a friend who has slayed his brand and his brag. Dan Babic is everything! He is tall, fit, Australian and fun! He works as an influencer and media personality, whose tag line (yes, he has a tag line) is, "*I didn't wake up to be basic.*" So, that statement alone tells you his brand. He wears Louis Vuitton and Tom Ford like it's his job, because well, it kind of is.

The way you communicate who and what you are matters. It needs to be clear in interviews and meetings. That doesn't mean it needs to be perfect your first time, but it should be well thought out. Don't just wing it. Have talking points, do your best, have tons of energy, watch it when you finish, and improve. I know it sounds cheesy, but you get to choose who you want to be every day of your life. Who says Hollywood doesn't have a heart? Well, I did, but that's beside the point. YOU are different! You get to stay human, even as you succeed. And you can succeed. You can apply these strategies to SLAY THE FAME GAME.

• •

Once you have mastered the five basic points to slay your humble brag, it's time to put them into a script. You'll need this every time you're on camera or meet someone while networking. You need to casually promote yourself. Emphasis on *casually*. No one likes an obnoxious advertisement that begs you to be interested. In other words, you need to keep the humble in the humble brag. Got it?

• •

Why don't you take a few minutes to write out your own humble brag? You can always edit later. Just go ahead and feel it out. Just make sure that whatever you say is 100% truthful and genuinely you. I mention Vogue in my humble brag because people respect you more when you have been validated by a person or organization they respect. One could also accurately assume that if Vogue covered me, there are many smaller outlets who have as well. Naming them all would be obnoxious. Just don't lie. DUH. That's the difference in famous and infamous. While I might be a hustler/workaholic, there are tons of people in Hollywood who talk big, but don't actually do anything. That makes it hard for people to sift through who truly has momentum around their brand, and who is just pretending. You want them to know you're legit.

WHAT'S THE POINT?

Being on camera is a great way to promote your brand. But don't get so wrapped up being the center of attention that you stray off topic. That is unless you have a charity to incorporate. I highly suggest finding a charity to work with early on. It's important not only because it will trend and work, but because it matters. This will give you purpose and keep you rooted in something important. It helps on those days when you're insecure, because you can just remember that it's not about you. It is about the people you're helping. Your time in the spotlight needs to do more than massage your ego. Find your purpose and use your platform to give voice to the voiceless. There's a bigger reason you're passionate about this industry. Find it, and commit to helping. Get fired up about human rights issues, bring a drama or arts day to schools, have

compassion for people living on the streets. Find the cause that speaks to your heart and get behind it. Maybe you have always loved animals. Become a spokesmodel for PETA or ASPCA. Find your cause and make a difference.

When you commit to being genuine, whether you're on the View or you're at the grocery store, you might discover parts of yourself you never knew. For example, maybe the reason you show skin is because you once had an eating disorder, and, after many years, have *finally* accepted your body as is. Do you see how quickly you just moved from someone people might judge as trashy to a spokesmodel who inspires others to live confidently and love their body? Find your why and fuel it.

Focus TV

⌜HOW DO INTERVIEWS WORK?⌝

Most on-air segments are seven minutes long. If you do them right, they fly by too fast. Usually, you'll arrive at the studio and be treated like the celeb you are. You'll be guided to the green room (aka a lounge for talent), where you can snack, zen out, drink water, get last looks (before you go on camera), etc. Most guest appearances require you to arrive camera-ready, so make sure you check before your close-up! Even if I'm on set with a makeup artist, I always bring my own stuff because I did a runway show once and the makeup was **HORRIBLE!** I had to fix it in the bathroom before I went on.

As soon as you arrive, you will likely have the showrunner/producer give you a rundown. Pay attention because they have done it three thousand times and will talk very fast. If you're on a radio show or podcast, the host may give you a few extra minutes before you go live or they hit record, but most of the time, your publicist will just patch you right through. If it is in studio, ask the show host to come by your green room before the show to introduce themselves and talk about the segment. While it is the polite thing to do, they might be too busy, so don't worry if they don't.

As soon as you arrive or pick up that phone, you want to be "on." I'm extremely quiet in the ride over to an interview or an appearance, but as soon as I walk in the door, I am "ON!" I give everyone my love, attention, and respect. I always have an assistant or two with me to take business cards, notes and behind the scenes footage. But, I only bring people with me who build me up and make me feel confident and funny! This is not the time for that judgy friend you can't seem to get away from. You need cheerleaders, positivity and fun!

84

Credit: Hamid Mosleh

From Prep to Perfection Tips to SLAY

Getting an interview is a BIG deal! Congrats, Queen! You should celebrate the fact that you're doing something right with all that pitching! Just don't celebrate *the night before* your big moment in the spotlight. Otherwise, those nerves will not be in good shape with little sleep and dark under eyes. Preparation is just as important as pitching. So, follow these tips and get ready for your close-up **ASAP**:

- Give your appearance some psycho power prep. Study the show host, show, specific segment you're featured in, and be prepared for the questions they will ask you.

- Practice with a supportive friend who will give you tips and encouragement. If possible, film yourself a couple of times and correct things you don't like.

- I'm the Queen of talking with my hands ... this is not a good thing on camera. But, it throws me off when I try to not do it. If you're a full-bodied talker as well, practice giving them a rest during normal convo by playing with a small jewel or ring. Focus on breaking the habit weeks before you go on camera, then forget about it. It's much worse to bomb your moment by worrying about those arms!

- If you're sharing advice or discussing a motivational topic, study up on statistics and research to back up your opinions and advice.

- Think of some icebreakers to use when you first mee[t] the host and producers, so you build a relationship righ[t] away. Just avoid politics and religion. Maybe try som[e] recent tech breakthroughs, sports (boring), news tha[t] isn't controversial, trending comedy videos, movie stars etc. Just make sure whatever you say is funny an[d] positive, not mean-spirited or rude.

- Start your morning with a healthy meal and workout Avoid carbs that make you tired. You need that boost o[f] confidence, energy, and glow.

- Take your time on hair and makeup, if you do it yourself I give myself at least two hours, so I feel relaxed and car[n] enjoy it. If possible, have it professionally done especially if your favorite makeup colors are bright blu[e] and pink ... in which case, we might want to have a littl[e] chat offline ..

Remember our style chapter? Make sure you have the perfect outfit. Avoid craz[y] patterns, black or big, flowy tops or dresses. The perfect outfit is in 'your' col[or] (ask a friend, if you don't know. Mine is red), flatters your body, is memorabl[e] and makes you feel like a Queen!

Remember that you're the expert, and what you're going to say can really ad[d] value to the audience. Don't let big sets, bright lights and stressed out producer[s] make you nervous. You belong here. You're born to SLAY.

Make SURE you know where you're going, especially if it's on a studio lot. Ther[e] are so many gates, your feet will thank you later if you take the time to confir[m] exactly where to go.

Give yourself PLENTY of time to get there. I always give myself an extra thirt[y] minutes to get wherever I'm going. That way, you can enjoy a peaceful wal[k] inside instead of a sweaty run.

If possible, avoid "umm, uh, nah, nope, yup" and one word answers during you[r] interview.

Be conversational, humble but confident. Focus on becoming friends with th[e] host on air. If they love you, their fans will.

- Remember that assistants can be strong allies, so treat them with the respect they deserve. Thank them for all their help.

- Understand the interview flow: 1) small talk on air to build a rapport and frame of reference (who are you) for the audience, 2) jump into the purpose of the interview: promote your project / get to heart of the matter, 4) wrap it up with a close and ask: "Check out my film on ___", "Buy my book on Amazon", "Follow me on my blog and social media."

- Know your main objective (sell books, promote the organization you support, promote your new web series), have your talking points ("My book, 'Slay the Fame Game', helps you break into entertainment without it breaking you! It was endorsed by Daily Mail and a famous actress from Pretty Little Liars. It encourages you when you feel like giving up!" and gently steer conversation in those directions. Whatever they ask you, it all comes back to your talking points. Memorize them. Know them. Share them ...

- Understand that sometimes you might not slay the way you want to. Sometimes there just won't be chemistry between you and the host. That's okay. Learn something, then move on.

- Follow up immediately with a thank you card and/or gift for the host and assistant.

- Promote the interview and share it on your social media channels.

- Add the interview to your media kit and website.

- Add the media contact to your spreadsheet.

Credit: Hamid Moslehi

SPEAK UP

People deal with nerves differently. Your host might be nervous. Don't rely on them to pump you up. You need to create your own energy. Don't let weird personalities sync you out. I had an interview with someone who had super weird energy. It could have thrown me off but I had learned how to speak up. This one was with a friend and producer who was very outspoken about her opinions of what I was saying. I felt myself shutting down emotionally. As a Scorpio, that's the worst thing that can happen on camera. I need my big personality on camera. Of course, every time I would say something, she or her partner would chirp in like an annoying little bird (not that birds are ever annoying) and say, "*Umm, nah, how about for that you say something more like ...*" Or, "*Yeah, I think you need to make sure what you are saying is really on brand because...*" While I assume they had good intentions, the constant nagging and poking just made me want to throw something and walk off. Of course, that would not have been the best way to manage my emotions. Fortunately, I found my voice and said, "*Hey guys, I know you have great intentions, but I'm sensitive, and every time you interrupt me to correct something I'm saying, you are shutting me down and I'm losing my energy. I'm guessing you want me to be 'on' for this segment, so will you just let me flow and answer the questions? If we need extra sound bites, I'm happy to grab them all at the end.*" Aren't I mature? It worked great. They freaked and apologized. No one wants to be the producer who killed the artistic energy in the room.

BE LOVE ON AND OFF CAMERA!

Credit: Britt Barrett

People don't relate to people trying, often desperately, to be famous. It comes off as thirsty. News flash, if your big dream is to be famous just to be famous, you're not going to be very likable in this world. There has to be a purpose to what you're doing.

You need to communicate your story and your why. Like everyone else, I had to figure out my why. I'm incredibly passionate about being the catalyst (or, at least a part of it) for people to find their inner potential and remove the blockers standing in their way. I also happen to have a unique skill at understanding the fame game in Hollywood and on social media. I can see problems, be direct yet encouraging and help others see the roadmap. All this directly explains why I would choose a public career that allows me to travel the world encouraging, educating and joking with entrepreneurial and creative Queens to help them reach their full potential.

Now, do you know what I just did there? I told you my story in an engaging way, that connects with your heart and shows how I can bring YOU value. Most people are wired to think, *"How does this affect me?"* What can I say? We are pretty selfish. That being said, it is important that your conversations are focused on why the person listening will care. Hopefully my story made you want to be my friend because that's all I've got. =)

Do you know why this matters in interviews? Because they are relationships at scale. And, some of the audience may have never heard of you. You may have told your story a million times, but today, you're talking to a random guy in Georgia who has never heard of you. If you speak with transparency from the heart, people will hear the sincerity and love you. That is unless you're a mean person, in which case, grab a therapist and come back to this in six months. JK! But, I will say, you can't slay entertainment long term if you haven't cleared the blockers in your heart and overcome your insecurities.

Credit: Stephanie Girard

Whether you live in Hollywood, or are slaying through social media in your bedroom, you must focus on being the very best person you can be. Success will come if you're doing what you love, being kind, working hard and believing in yourself. There's no need for a distracting Plan B if you know without a doubt that plan A is going to work. These concepts work because this industry is all about who you know. People are not going to want to know you if you're rude or acting out of insecurity. They want to see your heart. What is in your heart? Can you convey that in a way that speaks directly to theirs?

> Making people love you is not about fooling anyone. It is about finding who you are and being that Queen 100% of the time. I believe that we're all full of love from the moment we're born. We crave it, need it, we're even born from it. When people act like hater trolls, I think it hurts them more than their victim. It's not in sync with who they are.

How does that relate to Hollywood? Well, have you ever had someone bully or hate on you? Afterwards, were you inspired to help them out, give them your favorite Louis Vuitton or recommend them for a new internship? Of course not. That would be dumb. You might want to give them the opportunity to touch that LV bag ... as you whack them over the freakin' head with it (okay, don't do that). But, you wouldn't be inclined to help them out. I was giving someone some advice and she went on and on about how famous ... I'm not. Haha! It cracks me up because she didn't even realize she was being rude. Do you think I kept helping her? Now, imagine if she had shown gratitude and encouragement for my hard work to make it from trailer parks to red carpets? I already know I'm just north of the D list at times. If she had encouraged me as I try to pursue my dreams and help more people, I would probably feel more inclined to help her in any way possible. Building a rapport is the most fundamental tool in sales. If entertainment isn't sales, I don't know what is!

THE POWER OF A COMMON GOAL

Credit: Malachi Banales

One thing I've learned from watching my hubs launch over 200 successful film and TV show campaigns (okay, I haven't watched him launch all of them ... but you get it) is the power of a common goal. Let's say your passion is helping women with confidence, can you imagine the impact you could make if organizations who are also passionate about that helped you? They fundraise, host events, partner with celebrities and influencers and pitch to press on the daily. What if you called one of them up and told them your story? Shared your common goal? Imagine how impactful it would be if you joined forces and did interviews supporting them. Now, you're in the spotlight like you want, but you're actually helping people! You could become a role model and help make a difference. Plus, if you speak like I do, instead of just encouraging them one day then peacing out, you could connect them with an organization that could make an ongoing difference in their life.

To find the organization that fits, think about your purpose, then ask yourself, "*What are the largest organizations out there that focus on this topic?*" Reach out to them and see how you can help. Get involved, and let them know your goals and plans. Get on the board or committee, lean in to help. Contact celebs, press outlets, etc. on behalf of the brand. Those relationships might last your career lifetime. Always think of complete alignment. How can you make the greatest impact with the time, resources or experience you have?

DON'T FEAR A LITTLE SHOCK VALUE

Credit: Malachi Banales

There are many people in Hollywood who understand the power of shock value. You know the type. That reality star everyone hates ... but can't look away from. Love them or hate them, you're probably talking about them. Of course, that doesn't only apply to drama. It can be a bikini on a snowy day, a guy who eats his lunch in a dog bowl while sitting in a kennel with a starving dog too afraid to eat. Charities like **PETA** have even leveraged controversy, asking celebs to strip down in campaigns against fur. Don't believe everything you read.

I have been in the midst of my own controversies, but I have learned much more by helping my friends in the industry navigate them. I wish I could share more, but confidentiality agreements are pretty popular in Hollywood and nothing will scare your celeb friends more than a tell all. Just keep in mind, when you start down the fame game controversy rabbit hole, you're only worth as much as someone would pay for your last photo. Don't wreck your life over a feature that will sit on the front page for a few hours.

It's intimidating, but this industry is a ton of fun! I love it much more now than I ever did, because I get to create success on my terms. I don't have to worry about people telling me what to do or say. I get to be me 100%. That, in my opinion, is the difference in things working in this business and them not. Don't be afraid of making a few mistakes and having a lot of fun. Especially if **TMZ** is filming. They won't put you on air for your politically correct comment. They want to see you be human, make mistakes and be a little tongue-in-cheek.

I used to shy away because I had no clue who I wanted to be or what I wanted to be known for. But that would fall into the DON'T list. You know how they say 'those who can't do, teach'? Well, that was one of my dumb moments. I've since learned from my mistakes. Don't be afraid to put yourself out there. Be open to your brand evolution. Go for it with everything you've got. Be different. Don't be afraid to surprise people. Who cares if you make a mistake and have to apologize? Ignore the "should and shouldn't dos." Don't let some stupid excuse like fear hold you back. That's some of that whole "hindsight is 20/20" crap I learned. Fortunately, I learned it before it was too late to create a brand for myself in this business that I love so much!

CHAPTER 10

MAY REQUIRE MOCKTAILS: Networking

Let's say you're fresh off the Hollywood Greyhound (do those even run, anymore?) ready to take your career by storm. You're bright eyed, bushy tailed, and trying to find the right person to launch your career. Well, unfortunately, you're already thinking about this wrong! Eeek. I'm sorry. Don't worry, I won't judge but I will help. There isn't that one person who will launch your career. That is up to you! Sure, people will help ... a LOT. In fact, you'll be nowhere without them. But the work is up to you. You have to be out there shaking hands, getting photographed and looking fab. If you want to sit on your throne and wait for people to come up and help you, you're in trouble. You've got to get that gorgeous booty out there networking!

When I first moved to Hollywood, I didn't have a clue what networking was about. Fortunately, I'm a Southern girl who loves people. I may not have been networking, but I was definitely making friends. I didn't have an agenda and that helped me build awesome relationships. It didn't help me with business at first, but, years later when I launched The McCord List and started my shows, book, and events, they were incredibly supportive. Of course, prior to that, 'they had just known me as famous for being famous. Talk about slaying! Just kidding. That's actually not the best resume enhancement, but it was my reality at the time. I remember dodging the paps as much as possible because I had no clue what I was doing. I used to wonder how much easier it would have been for me to launch the career I have now out of that press attention, versus building it from scratch. But, I wouldn't have been able to write this book. I couldn't have related to the struggle and insecurities that come up when you are go at it on your own. I think we all need champions who cheer us on. My man is that person. I hope to be yours. I don't want you to look back like I did, thinking, "*GEEZ, Rach! What a waste of time!*" Fortunately, I learned before it was too late, but before I did ...

there was this...

Napa Valley for an Audi racing experience. It was a big jet, but we were only sharing it with Brittany Snow and her boyfriend (at the time), Ryan Rottman. I was actually pretty freaked about flying in a jet, versus the commercial flights normal people go in (i.e. me, the day before, and most days since). It's like a speed boat. You feel the bumps, but it kind of just glides right through them. It is a cool experience. Anyway! Once we arrived, we attended this "welcoming" event, where people basically did what they do in Hollywood. Get dressed up, take photos and hang around people they don't talk to. I use the words "hang around" pretty loosely. Because everyone just goes to their tables and sits quietly to themselves. If I had bigger balls, I would walk up to them and say something like, "*Hey, you know you aren't in solitary confinement, right? We can talk to each other, you know?*" Of course, that would be weird for a million reasons, one of which is that I actually do the same thing now. But, I'm just shy about approaching people. Southern belle, over here! I think other people should make the first move. Not just men, but that's just me.

The next morning, we arrived at the Sonoma Racetrack for training. It was an epic experience, especially if you're competitive, which I am. A group of fifteen celebs were all speeding along behind the professional racecar driver. I wish I could remember his name, but, again, this is networking gone wrong so that doesn't really shock me. My biggest concern was being the car right behind HIM (pro), because these cute actors were all too afraid to mess up their moneymaker. Not me! I just wanted to go as fast as possible. I hit 132 on a *very* complex track, which was about 30 mph slower than the pro. Not bad for a rookie, eh? Oh, and no, I'm not Canadian.

To this day, that's still one of my favorite Hollywood experiences yet. Talk about EPIC! It was put on by Muscle Milk and Audi and two of my friends, Jeremy and Shane McCassy. They are brothers and I just adore them.

Now, let's take a step back. Let's say I had read this book before attending and realized the importance of turning it into a good ROI (return on investment) for my time. Sure, it was still an epic experience, and I hear life is all about the experiences you have, but let's just say I was intentional about building and nurturing new relationships. What do you think I would have done differently?

For one, I would have chatted it up with Ms. Snow and we would have become BFFs. Then, at the welcoming event, I would have had a little mocktail to relax, and would have gone around making friends. Complementing them, asking about their flights and nerves about the next day, etc. Then, instead of focusing on being the fastest on the speedway, I would have focused on connecting with brand sponsors, featuring them on my blog, taking business cards and sending thank you notes. There isn't anything gross about that. It isn't thirsty networking. It's being relational. Having manners. That is what "networking" is all about. It's about building relationships. Not cashing in on someone, but to cash in together on something.

GET YOUR HEAD ON STRAIGHT

Credit: Malachi Banales

Let's say your dream is to be a reality star. Paid and famous for being your fab self ... Your number one goal is probably to network with producers and executives on shows that align with your goals, right? To do that effectively without being a user, you need to be the first one to bring value. Cover their shows on your blog, do features on them, introduce them to people they want to meet, invite them to events, etc. You can always find ways to bring value. I hand delivered bottles of wine to the producer of *Fashion Police* because she couldn't make it to one of my parties. In my head, the obvious thing to do was bring the party to her!

> If you created your own blog, when you meet your favorite celeb, producer, model, etc., you have a solid reason to talk to them. You can say something like, *"I loved your work on _____. I work as a _____, but I have a blog and would love to share a feature on you to my fans. They would love to hear your story! Are you interested?"*

Yass!! Now you are building a relationship. Praise emoji!!

Get creative. The power is in bringing value to the other person. Don't worry, I'll bore you with more of these examples later. The point to remember is this: get to the value QUICK. Whatever value you can bring to your ideal contact—in the earlier example, the fab producer of that show you dream of slaying—should be included in your back story. No offense, but Hollywood is too busy to care about your favorite color. But, if you bring value to someone else's life, no matter how busy they are, they will love you and your humble brag.

SLAY THAT HUMBLE BRAG

Do you remember us talking about your humble brag? This is important every time you meet someone. It matters in every interview, meeting, and conversation. I literally JUST used it on a flight I'm on. You never know who you're going to meet and when, so you need to always be ready to be "on." For example, let's say you were just hanging with a girl in Hollywood. You buddy up for a few minutes, then she asks what you do. You throw your humble brag out there, like a boss, and she is intrigued. She asks you to elaborate, and you SLAY your story, focusing on your biggest accomplishments and endorsements. But you don't sound like you're bragging at all. You're inclusive, current (with trending topics) and specific to what she might care about. This should come out in the beginning of your conversation. Now, why does this matter? Because, what if she then told you that she works as the assistant to Diana Madison, one of my favorites in Hollywood? Diana is a successful TV host with her own show. She knows how to SLAY when it comes to red carpet interviews, Hollywood topics, and juggling her personal life in the public eye.

This is yet another reason why being yourself is so important, on and off camera. You never know who you're meeting. Awesome, she likes you and introduces you to Diana for a potential interview. My man says business comes down to three things: **1) do I like you? 2) how can you help me rock? 3) prove you can do it.** For her to choose you for a gig or segment, she needs to know you can help her rock, by entertaining her fans. She wants them to LOVE you so they continue to LOVE the content on her show.

To slay **number one**, you need to build a relationship so she likes you. Compliment her, use your research of the show to compliment her work and have fun with her. If you never get past this spot, don't sweat it. If she knows you have chemistry and genuinely likes you, she will involve you when the opportunity makes sense. You don't need to go down the perfectly color coordinated checklist of things to cover in the meeting, if you're vibing and she loves you. People like to work with people they like.

To slay **number two**, she wants to know you're going to help her do what she does better. For on-air segments, she needs to know you're going to help with ratings (get more viewers, which leads to more advertising). Hollywood doesn't like taking big risks. They like to know that you trend, succeed, and kill it before they invest in you. But don't take that personally, it's just how the business works. Business comes down to generating results and producing return on investments.

For **number three**, it's important that you can show evidence that you have already SLAYED in the past. If you're thinking about some of our favorites on television, Bethenny Frankel, Wendy Williams, etc., they got their own show after they had successful shows under their Gucci belts. When fans respond well and ratings are high, networks will likely greenlight future shows. No one wants to tank 5 million in a show that is canceled after the pilot. On the other hand, if an actor has a lead role in a film, but it tanks at the box office, they might not get such a big chance again. Entertainment projects are like any other investment. People front cash and/or time with the hope of getting a return ($$) that far exceeds the investment. If not, it's a costly lesson they aren't likely to fail again.

Keep in mind, the talking about yourself should come after you've spent a good amount of time learning about your new friend. Don't be rude.

KEEP IT PERSONAL

Credit: Hamid Moslehi

Okay, you've slayed your humble brag, you've got the tips, you get the point, you know how not to act, now what? Well, that depends on who you're talking to. Be flexible and slightly shift your story based on the interest level. This is super important. I can't tell you how surprised I am when I overhear someone giving their (not so) humble brag in a way that doesn't even relate to the person they are talking to. Let's say I'm talking to the CEO of a company that sells cars. I'm sure at first glance it may seem like we have nothing in common, but I wouldn't be a hard-working Scorpio if I didn't give it a shot. Do you know what I would focus on with my humble brag? How I love to speak on topics to help brands promote themselves effectively or how I love helping people feel empowered to grow. Now, I have given him an excuse to potentially hire me for a motivational talk for his employees. Sure, he may pass but at least he knows what I do. Maybe he knows someone who might be interested. Just stay relevant to whoever you're talking to. Don't walk into a conversation about Hollywood talking about life as a waitress and don't walk up to a table of executives talking about being an actress, unless they are Mark Burnett, and you have practiced your humble brag a thousand times!

EVENTS ... WHAT'S THE BIG DEAL?

Credit: Kelly McKeever

The most uncomfortable event I've ever attended was my first gifting suite. It was so weird. I walked around a room, with a bunch of brand booths with product to gift celebs. Everyone is so nice, but if you aren't Angelina Jolie, they are asking who you are, and what they would know you from. It's so awkward. I almost want them to come out with it saying, *"Will you trend in press if I take a photo with you? I'm trying to decide if I should give you this $50 tea set or not."* I get it. The struggle is real. They work hard to build brands, spend money to attend these events and don't want to gift unless they are getting press. Of course, that means, even if you are someone who delivers press, you have to knock your ego down a few valves before you walk in. The perks are, you get prezies, meet new people and get press photos.

Now, in case you didn't dream of owning a brand-new onion slicer, what's the point? I wish I could be super profound, but we're talking Hollywood right now. The truth is, you go to be seen by the same people who were at the event you just left. They need to know you got invited and are popular. You laugh, but that's what New York Fashion Week is all about, unless you have a paid appearance. We also go to get photographed by press photographers. If you have a publicist pitching you, it's even better! Just make sure you carry your weight by looking GORGE. If you're covered in press often enough, in a short period of time you just might slay the hurdles and glide into consistent fame status.

When you attend events, you need to learn how to identify and approach the most important person in the room. Imagine every day in Hollywood is like those crazy job fairs at colleges. You need to diversify your time and focus on meeting the right people.

For the record, I hate this kind of stuff. I usually feel like a dork in a mismatched Chanel suit. I start sweating in all these weird places, I say dumb crap and daydream about Netflix and Chill. I'm kind of the worst at this. But, those who can't do, teach. Right? Eek. Just kidding ... ish. Do I love approaching new people? No, but, fortunately, there comes a point in your career when you don't really have to do it as much. I'm not saying you never do, but it definitely becomes easier, because you now know more than half the room, so it is full of casual introductions from friends, versus the awkward: *"Hi, I'm Rachel."*

Own That Party, QUEEN!

Credit: Adam Kay

Part of owning that party is being seen. Of course, when most celebs go out, they usually sit in the back or in a **VIP room**, facing the wall, talking low, trying not to be bothered. But, when you're getting started, aka don't yet have fans harassing you, you want (and **NEED**) to be seen all the time. In fact, when you attend events, you need to think of cheesy reasons to do a dramatic lap (or five) around the venue to meet everyone. Oh, and if you sit, make sure you're facing the entrance. Laugh, look fabulous and slay girl, slaaay.

I know it sounds cheesy, and you're probably judging me ... especially if you too have a successful career in Hollywood. But, you know I'm right. And, as corny as I sound and as much as you want to call me up to tell me I have issues, you know I'm right. This book isn't called 'slay the obscurity game' for a reason. When people see you everywhere, all the time, the grassroots perspective says you're legit. Sorry, it's true. Unless you're that girl who is just making out with all the security guards to get into the party. In which case, we know that too. Eek.

Sure, being out constantly, when you really just want to binge watch, well, anything, is hard. Trust me, my heels hurt after my nightly five events. But, it is all about positioning. Fame is just marketing done extremely well. You're marketing yourself by slaying the fame game. That gives you the power to sell whatever you want. If you have the audience, you have the power. Research varies, but most marketing geniuses (like my man) will tell you that it takes 6-13 touch points with a potential customer before they buy. For example, they need to see/hear about a brand in social media, on a billboard, through email, through a friend, on radio, etc., a total of 6-13 times before they will buy whatever it is selling. In this case, you're the product, that means you need all these touch points with editors, fans, producers, etc. You need to pop up on their radar enough times to build familiarity and interest. All joking aside, that is the strategy behind all these events and all this work we do to slay the fame game and own that party.

THE ANXIETY IS REAL ... NOW GET OVER IT

Now that you have legit examples of how to connect and build friendships in the industry, I thought we should talk about the thing on every introvert's mind. HOW do I just *talk* to them? If you're like me, and hate making the first move, I feel you. I feel like a psycho, looking around to see who I should talk to. I want networking to be strategic. I also want it to be relaxed and fun. Who says it can't be? Sure, your anxiety might be kicking but hang in there. When you ease into networking it's a lot easier to enjoy the process. Remember, you don't need to meet *everyone,* especially when you're just starting out. The key is to meet *someone.* I know, unless you're an extrovert, this is still scary. I get it. The anxiety is real. But anxiety can't hold you back unless you allow it. Because I was homeschooled, I hated talking to new people. It wasn't something I really did that much, except with other people in my homeschool group. And, I'm not going to say they were weirdos ... but let's just say we weren't talking pop culture. I was, and will forever be, a nerd on the inside. Of course, at a certain point in my career, I realized I had to start being confident and actually finishing my own sentences. Yes, that's right. This loudmouth most people recognize as a total extrovert was once a scared little thirteen-year-old who couldn't finish her own sentences. So, how did I go from that nerdy girl with big knees in trailer parks to one of the most well-connected people in Hollywood? I decided to put myself in uncomfortable situations on the daily. I developed a character for myself. Built up my confidence and started pushing myself. I started giving myself permission to be me. No judgment. Once I stopped being afraid of messing up and being judged, I started having more fun and people actually started liking me more. I didn't want to change on the outside, I wanted a full body change. Now I'm honest about my insecurities and people tell me they were feeling the exact SAME thing! I love it!

NEVER BURN A BRIDGE

The moment you jump into the fame game you might feel a little insecure. Your outfits might not feel good enough, which, if we're honest, mine weren't. Then, as soon as you make it and your career takes off, it's easy to feel terrified that someone or something might cause it to unravel. It doesn't help that you have a million people lined up behind you to take your place. This isn't the town to make mistakes. Because if you insult the wrong person, act like too much of a diva, or forget to be grateful, you're in trouble.

It doesn't take long to be replaced in this industry. Plus, you never know where that person (aka bridge) might end up. For example, imagine if you failed to deliver on something you promised, snapped at someone or created pointless drama with someone ... just to find out they are best friends with or switched jobs to become the director on the film you want to book. Oops. That could be awkward. It would suck if that choice gets in the way of your first paycheck in Hollywood. It's a lot of work to land that first check. It probably took at least a hundred auditions. Which, by the way, I still complain about. Why can't you just watch an actress' reel and hire them or not? Book us direct, duh. Do we really need to go through all that freaking anxiety for an audition when they could have saved us all a lot of time by checking out our skills or non-skills on tape? It seems *painfully* inefficient. Emphasis on the painfully. Or at least come to the lobby and point out the ones who look the part and send the rest of us hopefuls home? Okay, enough of my Rachel rant. There actually is a point to all those auditions full of competitive side glares in the lobby and parking tickets on the side streets. Because every time you read for a casting director, you are getting more experience and, as long as you don't burn a bridge, they might remember you from an audition and bring you back for the perfect role!

DON'T WASTE YOUR DIAMONDS ON DOUCHES

While you should never burn a bridge, you should also never waste your diamonds on people that don't respect you. And, when networking like it's your job—because, it kinda is—you will meet them. Trust me. If there's one thing I have less than an ounce of tolerance for, it's people who want to bring others down or grumpy people who expect you to work hard to impress them. It's like they just sit there waiting for you to convince them that you're interesting, entertaining, and talented enough to be successful. Umm, no thanks! Remember when to exit well ... i.e., NOW. I had someone tell me that I will have a hard time breaking into any industry without a college education. Well, hate to say that I love to say, *"Look at me now, love!"* Can you believe the *outrage?* A girl without a college education writing a book, speaking at schools like UCLA, having her own show, and starting two companies. Too bad we all know she will NEVER read this book. LOL! Oh well, at least my ego got her moment. When you walk up to someone who thinks they are better than you, keep on walking. That would be one of those douches. Know your worth and believe in yourself. I know multimillionaires who didn't finish high school. Do I recommend skipping school? Of course not! But, don't let anyone tell you that you can't do anything. Just respond with something like, *"That might be true for you but not for me!"* Then, believe in yourself with all your heart!

> Don't waste your time trying to win those people over. Respect yourself enough to walk away. You attract where you are in life. So, keep life positive and beautiful.

Featuring the lovely,
Eva A Catherine

CHAPTER 11

SQUAD GOALS: Collaborations

I have a friend in Hollywood named Heidi Nazarudin "TheAmbitionista." She is a go getter, FABULOUS woman. I'm literally obsessed. Similar to my community of influential tastemakers, The McCord List, she started Blogger Babes to support her tribe. As our brands began to grow, everyone kept telling me I needed to meet her. Most would think we would be competitive, because it sounded like we were doing similar things, but, just as soon as I thought that, I pushed it out of my head. Everyone raved about her, and I wanted to meet her.

However, in our business, busyness is a way of life. Gosh, I remember being single (and not an entrepreneur) and reading a meme that said: "Busy' is code for a-hole." Sorry Queen of memes, that's just not (always) true. Being busy doesn't make you an a-hole, it makes you a BOSS b*!ch. That was the deal with Heidi and me. It took over six months for our calendars to line up. And, I'm pretty sure she loves me as much as I do her.

Finally, we connected after a Hollywood luncheon I was moderating and hosting with NAMI

(National Alliance for Mental Illness). She was so sweet and had amazing energy. Of course, it took us another seven months to hang again. Then, another four after that. Now, we're pitching a TV show and co-hosting events.

Being capable of doing the work is not only amazing and respectable, it's *necessary* for success. Waiting on someone else to carry the weight will get you in trouble. But, once you have a legit value/brand in business, partnering with the right people helps that success multiply.

Think of how much more you can do with the support of someone else. If you co-host an event, it can elevate each brand and build more momentum. Even if you invite some of the same people, it only encourages more interest because "everyone is talking about it." If you and a friend each have 500,000 fans with similar brands, collaborate on a project and watch your fan base grow. It's the most obvious and necessary choice for success. Don't waste time demanding all the spotlight. You can either build fifteen minutes of fame or a fifteen-year career. It's up to you.

HOW TO COLLABORATE

So, how do you do it? It's important to bring as much if not more value than you are looking to extract. For example, if you're contacting another influencer with a larger following than you, why not offer to bring in a photographer and/or videographer to shoot? Or if you really want to make a splash, why not get a few girls together and shoot something like my Vanity Fair inspired photoshoot? We had twelve influencers and entrepreneurs decked out in gorgeous Oscars gowns for a photoshoot. The brand collaborating with us provided hair, makeup, photography, gowns, tanning and gifts. We had the best time and got tons of exposure from it.

I shoot a podcast weekly and have all my close friends on it. It's a blast! Content creators need content. If you help them get it, they will adore you. Even if you don't have relationships with them yet, put something together and reach out.

HOW TO REACH OUT

When you reach out, come with friendly, "*I've known you forever*" energy. Comment on how much you love their work, then ask if they're interested in collaborating. Get to the point quickly. Don't send a long email. They are probably busy, so don't take it personally if they don't respond. Just kindly follow up. Don't be rude. I recommend something like this:

Hi _____!

How are you? You are so beautiful! I really love following your work. Congrats on all the success. You inspire me so much!

I'm reaching out because I'm hosting a photoshoot in _____ next Saturday from 12-3PM. I'm providing drinks, snacks, photography, hair, and makeup! Would you like to come by? It will be a blast! We already have _____ coming.

I know we haven't met before, but I'm new to the industry, and have been collaborating with some fabulous other creatives. I thought this would be the perfect way to create content and network with other fabulous ladies, like you!

Let me know if you would like to pop by! My cell is _____.

XO

Celeb connections are very similar. They, too, are human ... I mean, that should be obvious. While it is harder to email them directly (unlike bloggers, they are not putting their email address out for the world to see), you may meet them at an event or appearance. Say hello, compliment them, strike up a convo, ask questions, listen, care, be interested in what they are interested in. Get to their passion quickly and you might find yourself wrapped up in a stimulating conversation that lasts for hours.

Credit: Johnny Chicollo
Featuring the lovely, Eva A Catherine

If you come up with a solid reason to connect afterward (feature on your show, an introduction, etc.), it's normal to exchange contact. Maybe you didn't connect, but something comes up that you think might interest them. You can pull the email address for their people from IMDb or Celebrity Intelligence and reach out. Let's say you work at a gorgeous restaurant; why not contact their people and offer a complimentary dinner and transportation? You never know, they might say yes.

Another great reason to get involved with anyone in the industry is to support charity. We all have heart projects and sometimes we just want someone to support us with them. Most publicists work on promoting TV shows and film projects, but their charities and passion projects are often ignored. Volunteer, host an event, help them fundraise.

PROMOTE OTHER PEOPLE

One thing our industry needs more of is positive encouragement! We need to promote and support other Queens doing what we do. Stop being afraid of competition and start helping out! Not only will it make their day, it's good karma. Support other ladies in the industry, and don't be afraid to share the spotlight. It makes me happy every time I see my favorite ladies together. Plus, when you have other fabulous people on board, it legitimizes what you're doing.

You could also collaborate with social media giveaways. Fans love these because, I mean, who doesn't love fabulous presents?! As discussed in the chapter on social media, giveaways are a great way to grow. But, they are an even better way to collaborate with other fabulous creatives.

Here's how it works. Each of you post at the same time, and you create a circle for fans to follow. They are encouraged to "follow + like" an image, then go to the next profile and do the same. The go around until they make it back to the original page. Just don't have too many people involved because that can be so annoying!

BLOG FEATURES

Social media posts get lost but SEO (Search Engine Optimization) is forever. Why not trade some shout-outs on blogs or pay to get some stories that create a buzz? This is a great way to grow a following and look more legit to Google.

Plus, if you walk into a big meeting tomorrow, the first thing they do when you leave is Google or Bing you (just kidding, no one uses Bing), to see how legit you are. I had just pitched a new business partner on working together last week and a few days later I was covered by Snapchat in a big feature. He reached out and said, "Whoa, I didn't realize how legit you are! You popped up in my feed without me ever looking! We need to work together." Now imagine if the first ten pages of a Google search results in blog posts from hundreds of interviews talking about you? They will know they should work with you. Because, well, they should.

I have a little industry secret, it's called Fiverr. It is a freelance database of people around the world who will do practically anything for a small fee, starting at $5. It is unheard of but true. Imagine if you hired an admin assistant for a couple hours to help you pitch bloggers? Or, even better, you hired a blogger to cover you? Next level thinking. Sure, you can tell people how fabulous you are, but why not have someone else do it?

TIPS TO REMEMBER

When contacting someone new, be prepared with your "logline". A short but compelling description of who you are and why they should care. For example, if you're reaching out to a stylist you have dreamed of working with, get to value proposition as quickly as possible. You need to know your strengths and communicate them quickly. Think of how you can help first.

Your entire career doesn't rely on one person. Don't stress if they don't respond or they turn you down. Keep going—it's a numbers game. Be genuine in each interaction. Don't gush about stuff you couldn't care less about. Find something they do that you love and tell them.

Remember your value. It's easy, when you meet someone like Steven Spielberg, to feel inadequate. Don't! You're a fabulous queen with tons of value. Meeting someone with amazing talent, wealth, success, and/or fame doesn't diminish your value. It makes you a Queen who just met someone with amazing talent, wealth, success, and/or fame.

One of the best lessons I wish someone had taught me was you don't have to know everyone, you need to know the right one(s). You need an epic team who believes in you, some powerful media supporters and fabulous friends to share life. Don't be so focused on spreading wide that you forget to go deep with the people who matter. Don't get so busy with BS you forget to succeed in the business.

If you want to SLAY THE FAME GAME you need to become BFF with the right people. Stay kind and friendly with everyone and don't waste time with the wrong people. Every person you work with should have a bigger platform than you. They should also have a similar brand/following, so their fans want to follow your work too.

105

CELEB SQUATTERS

Having celeb alignment is obviously great for your career. In fact, it is so great, most people will settle right into plus one status ... as a full time mooch. Eww. I am literally rolling my eyes. Don't be a celeb squatter. By the way, I didn't even want to write this section, but celeb alignment has helped so many people SLAY THE FAME GAME, so I knew you'd be wondering. Just keep in mind I have had personal experiences with celeb squatters ... when I wasn't the one they were eyeing. So I had a bad taste in my mouth.

Here's the deal, it sucks when people you knew before they were famous get hit with Hollywood, and your relationship changes because of it. It also SUCKS when celeb squatters use someone because of their well deserved success. In business, entertainment, life, whatever. Unfortunately, it happens WAY too much. BUT that doesn't make it excusable. I have had many people climb all 5'9 (okay, 5'8.5) of me to get to my people. I actually feel bad for both of them. The celeb ends up used and the user shows they obviously don't respect themselves. Hell, I've even felt bad for myself, who ends up feeling like a poor girl's <insert celeb name here>. Yes, it's weird watching people weasel in from every corner, trying to position themselves closer to your friend than you. It's annoying really. But, I'm not the one to judge the celeb worshippers who pop up out of nowhere. But I am the one to get away from them!

It's a lose, lose (yourself) situation. So, don't go pitching a tent in some celeb's vajayjay and roasting marshmallows up there just yet. It's gross to use someone for their celebrity status and it's even grosser to lose yourself in the process. Don't be a mooch, respect yourself and their heart enough to build true friendship with people you truly love. Where or not they are successful.

EXCLUDE THIS GIRL FROM THE SQUAD

I met this girl who I liked right away. She had a fun, 'tell it like it is' vibe about her, and I really enjoyed her company. Unfortunately, I got the feeling she was using me. She would poach all of my friends and ask for favors on the daily. This was not a collaboration, it was more like a one-sided delivery service. When you have to be "on" ALL the time, the friends you surround yourself with during your off time need to be *true* friends. You don't get that with people who are trying to use you. I need real friends with whom I can close the curtains, grab a bag of Cheez-Its, and turn on my favorite show.

Anyway, long story short, she freaked out on me at my house one night saying she didn't want to waste time with me when I wasn't introducing her to my influencer and celeb friends. *"UMMM, OKKKKKKAYYYYYY B, this is NOT working out. I literally have zero interest ... Oh, and can you please leave my remote on your way out?*

The moral of the story is to clearly define if you are friends, boss Queens or both. If you go with option C, make sure you're bringing equal value alongside that list of requests. Oh, and understand the limitations on what they can give. Don't guilt or blame them for their inability to hang. Respect that they might be extremely busy and probably have lots of pressure on them. Cut them slack, focus on your own work, and remember it's your responsibility to work the hardest on your career. Oh, and if they are using you, and you're unhappy, make sure you walk away ... and delete those digi

THE CELEB DON'T LIST

Just for fun, I thought I'd share a (obvious) list of DO NOTs on things to NEVER say or do to a celeb:

"*Oh my gosh, I'm so obsessed with you!!! You have no, no* (between hyperventilation), *no idea how much I love you. I need you. Oh my gosh!! Can we be BESTIES??? I'll give you anything you want.*" Never do any of that. Duh. Or any version of that. Obviously. Be as "normal" as possible and play it chill. Not weirdly chill ... just middle chill. Have kind, friend energy. Of course, if you do anything, even somewhat like the above, you might not get your bestie but you'll probably get a restraining order. YAY! Their legal name will be on it and everything.

"*I know this may sound a little crazy (yes it does) but I'm ready to settle down and I think you are the one. You've just really have everything I look for. I remember watching you on Jimmy Fallon, and Ellen, and Kris Jenner—well, before her show was canceled, I even remember when you did that cast interview ... when you were three. You and I are meant to be together.*" Don't say this to anyone. Celeb or otherwise. Ever. Enough said.

"*Hey! I've been reading this epic book, SLAY THE FAME GAME* (you can say that part, just not this

Credit: Alphie Chikwashi

one ...), *and Rachel encouraged me (to be clear, that is not what I'm doing) to find a celebrity so I can be famous! Yay. Would you like to be that lucky someone? I make great eggs every morning!*"

P. S. you might want to hide this book if you make a lot of celeb friends. Well, after you finish reading it. Don't throw it away, though ... 'cause that would be lame ... *and I'll come find you* (**Wedding Crashers** style) ...

CHAPTER 12

Ewwww, let's talk about HATERS! Here's what I have to say about those little human trolls ...

<Tear this out in case you run out of toilet paper>

THE WORST HATERS AKA YOUR "FRIENDS"

If there's one type of hater that really bums me out, it is (ex) close friends. Honestly, that's the one that really baffles me. I've always been the type of person who loves bringing people together to succeed ... squad goals style. If I have a shoot going on, the first thing I want to do is involve my friends. Or someone needs an introduction, I always connect them. I just think it is the normal thing to do. Unfortunately, a lot of people don't operate that way in this industry. So watch out for the ones who never want to help or encourage you. Eww. This industry should be fun and collaborative! Oh, and to the ones afraid to share the spotlight, media actually prefers stories of BFFs over the tiny brain haters and their loney shadows. It is much more interested to talk about multiple people, and how they engage together. I.e. where they are at, what they are doing, etc. Gigi meet Kendall style. Bottom line, if you're going to follow my track in this book, please follow this: do NOT turn into a selfishly ambitious queen who doesn't care about anyone else. Become a QUEEN who loves everyone

Credit: Alphie Chikwashi

and truly wants to use their her platform for good. Trust me, this town is small. If you are a B (and I don't mean Beyoncé), people will find out about it. It will show in the way you talk, carry yourself, etc. If you make EVERYTHING about you and forget about the people who love you, they will forget about you. But, more importantly, you'll become another gross hater. Which basically means this chapter will refer to you. Save us all some time and don't sip the haterade.

SHOW THEM THE DOOR... SLAM

You wouldn't think I would write this under the HATERS chapter because we started off sooo good ... but Hollywood happened! I become friends with a FABULOUS Queen. We were besties who would do everything together. She was pretty, fun, and crazy, but she was my best friend and I loved her! After a couple years, we started to drift apart. You know where this crazy train is heading ...

109

She began dogging my career, acting weird, and not showing up at my events. It really hurt my feelings because she was always super sweet to me, but something changed. It wasn't until she went went 51 shades of crazy that I realized we couldn't be friends anyone. Basically, we had gone up for the same job and I booked it. I have always been the kind of person to be happy for my friends' successes, but it was really bothering her. I zoned out for one second, and all the sudden she is commanding me to turn down the job. Well, if there's one thing you should know about me, it's that you should never *command* me to do anything. I mean, if you came in with guns blazing telling me to eat Pinkberry (which I love), I would still say no. To the crazy all things are insane, so

Credit: Stephanie Girard

after the mental meltdown, I started distancing myself. Not even intentionally. I don't like unpredictability and this had become just that.

I was bummed that she decided to throw our friendship in the blender over a modeling gig, but that wasn't the worst part. It was when she took it a step further trash talking me to everyone she could get her iPhone lips on that really sent it over.

So, what's the point of the story, other than the obvious need for a therapeutic release? Even with the best of intentions, as much as you may try to avoid it, you're going to have crazy situations pop up in this industry. Someone is going to turn on you or turn on the haterade. The key here is to 1) protect yourself (i.e. remove yourself from hateful, disrespectful, unsafe, or unpredictable situations), and 2) alternate between processing and avoiding the situation. Then, only when you're ready, 3) decide how you want to move forward in a way that brings you peace. Peace has to be the goal. Avoid the crazies or jelly "friends" who go psycho. Don't waste your time stooping to their level. Just talk some time away (I say three days if you are really upset), and decided how you want to handle hiccups like this. Whether you want to confront it or ghost her, it is your choice. Just don't hang around when someone makes you feel like crap! That goes for people you date as well. You only live once, don't waste it visiting your haters at the psychc ward.

The important thing to avoid is stooping to their level of nuts. Fighting fire with fire doesn't work in relationships. Create healthy boundaries in your life and be assertive enough to know when someone needs to be shown the door. Then, if necessary, you can give it a little slam. Peacefully, of course. :)

LET'S CALL THOSE TROLLS OUT ... SHALL WE?!

Credit: Hamid Moslehi

Ewwwww. These are probably the most inexcusable. Trolls with no balls. People outside Hollywood assume we have perfect little lives but in reality, we deal with so much of the same crap everyone else does. Hollywood / social media is like high school × 10,000,000. However, instead of bullies who pick us apart in the locker rooms, we have nameless, fameless trolls, with creepy screennames saying the meanest things they can muster up. They are little hater cowards who think their lives in their moms' basements have equipped them with enough wisdom to appropriately hate on us. Awww, aren't they cute!?

Seeing as how most of these little tools want to stay hidden, I found that to be the perfect reason to call their little crap out. Please note, I would happily sit down with any one of my haters, however they like to hide behind hateful words and masked IP address. So, why not call them out right here in my book? Want to hear the kind of BS bullying I get online? Of course you do! Let's do this!

- Tony, Up North said: Hell of a body, blimey! – *Thanks, but I'm not bulimic, a- hole.*

- Frankieboy, Stockton said: Looks around the 19 mark, pushing 30? *Really?—Umm, does anyone know what that means? I am old ... I guess?*

- Skofod said: You could use that nose as an excavator at a dig site.—*I get it, you think I have a big nose. Should I get surgery and change who I am because you don't like it? What was your name again?*

- Compaid, Warrington said: not a good look.—*I agree, your masked face is much prettier. Thanks!*

- Barryj, On an island, Bahrain said: She is starving herself.—*Great point. Can we discuss this over In-N-Out? Or my homemade mac & cheese, please?*

- My Pointless Views, Portsmouth said: Nice close shave there Rachel! - *Wow, did you really just zoom in on my pits to see if I had any imperfection? Wow, and we thought you didn't have a life! Agreed, this is a "pointless view."*

- Gildorg said: Yeah, and the loser of the family makes an appearance...—*It's a good thing we have you ... the non-loser to create an account on Daily Mail so you could accurately call me the loser in the group ... as I shoot my modeling campaign.*

- Blumpenkump said: Her face looks like it hit every branch on the ugly tree on the way down, but her a** is very bangable. This is a conundrum.—*Thank you ... I guesssss? Why don't you start working at 13 to get yourself out of trailer parks and into a better life? That way we can all sit back and judge you, your face, and your career when you finally get to become more than you thought possible for yourself.*

111

Mr. Rightt, United Kingdom said: Butterface—*Well, I am so happy we cleared that up! Now, where is that paper bag for my face?*

Major Woody, San Francisco said: It's like 70 degrees in Los Angeles and she's in a bikini! Look at me! Look at me!—*Well, technically, that was what wardrobe provided me to wear for my photoshoot ... but sure. You can look, if you'd like!*

Dragonfly, Birmingham, United Kingdom, said: Body's amazing, face is just average—*Thank you for clarifying. I wasn't 100% sure.*

As you see, we all deal with this crap. It is sad and annoying, but don't let it get to you. The truth is, you have to be pretty down in your life to either judge or feel jealous of every other human in the world. When you love life, and live it to the fullest, you won't waste your life putting someone else down. The sad truth is that a lot of people point their fingers at everyone else because they have nothing else to do with their hands. It makes me sad for them. I want a world full of love and kindness. One where we help instead of hurt. That's why, even though I'm no pushover, I actually have compassion for them. I hope that every person out there who hates himself enough to spread non-love will one day put all that energy into creativity, love, kindness. If they did, their lives would improve greater than they think possible!

On a side note, I've gotta be honest, some of their comments were pretty witty (to use a Christine Peake approved UK word). They obviously have a sense of humor so maybe they should stop judging and start doing. Hell, maybe they should read my book and SLAY THE FAME GAME for themselves.

YOU'VE FOUND YOURSELF ON THE WRONG SIDE OF A JOKE ... NOW WHAT?

I didn't get to a place of eye rolls versus fetal position crying over hater trolls overnight. It hurt ... a lot ... for a while. I can't say it doesn't still bum me out sometimes ... I mean, I could, but that would be lie, so I won't. The key is feeling the emotion then letting it go. Not *after* you get plastic surgery. Right now. Just because a troll has two upside-down thumbs and an index finger doesn't mean he or she can pull you down. Not unless you let them. That's why you need to stay confident and powerful, no matter what. Now, if someone in your inner circle does it, it's time to give them the boot. Sorry! Life is too short to allow people to intentionally tear us down.

If you have someone on your team giving advice that sometimes hurts, that's a different story. They might be trying to help. My man is the most amazing encourager ever. He is always on my side and helping me through the ups and downs of life and Hollywood. But, he will, occasionally, give me a slice of humble pie. I'll be like, "*Ummm ... thanks*? ..." Of course, I know he has my best interests at heart. But, I have had people close to me use our hang sessions as excuses to tell me what's wrong with my hair, outfit, ideas, work ... I even had one say, "Can you even spell that?" when I told them I was an entrepreneur!!! Deep breaths.

Don't let these people steal your joy. The first thing to ask yourself is, is this coming from a good place? Sometimes, the answer is yes. For example, if they say, "*Hey you look so beautiful but let me grab that roll of toilet paper you are dragging*," they are helping. If they say, "*Umm you aren't that talented*," you should bounce—they are being a hater.

I use the future / present versus past system. For example, if someone is saying something to help me do what I'm currently doing or will do better, I find that helpful. Unless they are trying to tell me to just give up obviously. But, if they are just trying to dig on something I did, like whoa, that shoot you did is so ugly or you looked so crazy in that outfit ... it's RUDE.

WANT YOUR POWER BACK? JUST TAKE IT

Credit: Alphie Chikwas

In order to get away from stepsister syndrome friends (straight out of Cinderella), I had to get uninterested in crap they would say about me. If you care about the drama, you'll find it. I don't read comments, the lips of trash talkers, or intercept disses. Who cares!? So what if they hate me? There are over seven billion people in this world. Do I really need to change because one person doesn't like me?

I remember being out in a big personality/loud talking group (myself included). To me this a normal Monday through Sunday. To get a word in my house (over Rick, my two chihuahuas or me), you need to talk loud and push through. We definitely aren't that family that has afternoon tea with a side order of silence. We bring it. So, this girls' night was like any other day in my life. But, apparently, we had a quiet one among us. Of course, I didn't notice her (because she was so quiet), but she was starting to fume. I mean, she must have had something important to say but after waiting for however long to speak, she hit purple rage and screamed: "UMM!! EXCUSE ME!!! CAN YOU GUYS SHUT UP SO I CAN SAY SOMETHING!?!" While I understand the feeling, I don't personally relate. If I have something to say ... it gets said. I don't wait for anyone else to give me permission. My response, in the suddenly awkward room, was, "*Honey, if you want to say something, just say it.*" The same is true with power. If you don't want to give your power away to haters ... DON'T. Give them respect, love, and kindness ... then give them your back as you WALK away!

It's about having a thick skin, yet not about being an ice Queen narcissist. It's about accepting yourself so if you read a mean comment you can think, "*Yup! So what?*" I know I have a big nose. So what? It's mine and I love it. By one person's standards it might not be perfect, but it's perfect for me. That's why it is on MY face. God chose it and I think He is smarter than whoever that nameless troll was. Just because someone has an opinion doesn't make it true or untrue. It just makes it that: their opinion. Should I change because one person in a world hates it? Of course not! Forget the haters. Focus on loving and accepting yourself.

TAKE THAT, HATERS!

Before I call "episode wrap" on this fun chapter, I HAVE to share my system on responding to jealousy hate. I invite them to sit in their moment. You know when someone says, "*Whoa girl, your makeup looks CRAZY! Hahahahah,*" my response is, "*Really, why do you say that?*" Most of the time haters want to "pretend" they're joking, as they insult you up and down. If you hang with people like that, remaining oblivious to all the haterade, you'll suddenly feel down and upset. Well, not on my watch! The key is to bring awareness to their rudeness. Maybe you grew up with an aunt who has always put you down. You never noticed it because it was so "normal." Once you become aware, you realize why you never liked hanging with her. When you bring light to the girl fight, you can face it head on. Some people are straight up bullies. But "friends" hide it behind sarcasm. That's why, when they insult you, if you ask them straight out, "*Why do you say that?*" they will be held accountable for the passive aggressive shade they are throwing. After being called out few times, especially in front of people (if that's how they insulted you), they will wake up. Girl, bye.

MAKE THEM LOVE YOU: Build Your Team

Having an epic team that supports you will completely change the game. Look, I didn't have a team knocking on my door, doing my makeup and pulling me into photoshoots and meetings when I first started out. You probably won't either. But don't worry! If you do a great job building your brand and slaying the fame game (which you will), you won't have to be a one-woman circus for long.

My man was the first one to believe in me ... long before I did. There's something about growing up in trailer parks that makes you feel like a loser who should fly under the radar. I still can't believe I have a life in the public. We're talking about the girl whose first brand logo had her completely hidden under a hat. It's still weird sometimes. I'm so grateful but sometimes I just want to hide out. Fortunately, I'm not the most famous person in the world so I can ... pretty easily. =)

Credit: Stephanie Girard

Having a fab team helps me stay consistent when I feel like giving up. Rick taught me what it means to build and protect a brand. Next thing you know, it took off so I started helping friends in the industry do the same. Before long, I had squeezed eight years in entertainment into SLAY THE FAME GAME, had my own show, direct model bookings and community in Hollywood. Now, I have an amazing team around me! Rick introduced me to FABULOUS women like Whitney and my twin soul Esther at The Fedd Agency, and their belief in me changed the game. Suddenly, I was meeting the head of FOX, in pitch meetings with people calling this the next #GirlBoss (of course I feel totally unworthy), and flying across the country for meetings and events. Having people who believe in you and support you helps you go from BASIC to BEYOND!

Instead of going at all this alone, I have amazing people who want to see me succeed. I may be a workaholic in my own right, but nothing I can do compares to what can be done when you have the right people with you. Like attracts like. Boss Queens attract Boss Queens. And positive people attract positivity. So, if you crawl out of bed at 12PM, only focusing on looking as cute as your body allows, we probably won't be working together anytime soon.

I wake up with a non-caffeinated charge every morning, asking myself, "*What am I focusing on? What am I going to achieve?*" By the time I started this book, everything Rick and I had done to build my brand was without an agent or a manager. When I hear people say, "*I can't do anything without an agent,*" it bothers me. Of course you can! That kind of limited thinking keeps you stuck.

It is a partnership, even after you find the right team. If you're waiting on the paycheck to start building experience or an agent to start the hustle, you're in trouble. You should be networking constantly slaying the fame game, and actively researching new projects. Sure, some agents might get annoyed, but the right one will respect your hustle. Plus, imagine how much easier it would be for them if you compiled a list of emails and contact names for projects you want to work on? Just always check with them first to make sure you aren't overstepping. And always have gratitude for everything they do.

MY FIRST TEAM WASN'T RIGHT

Remember I told you people are fake in Hollywood? Good. Then, you should also remember me telling you I suck at that. I'm talking my DNA rejects that crap. I remember when I started modeling, getting signed by a modeling agency in Georgia. I was so excited ... well, that is until my Scorpio sense realized I was working with a PSYCHO! I'm talking certifiably ... INSANE. Rude, demeaning, crazy, etc..I would call his office to check in and it was like interrupting an anger management class. It did not go well. The assistant was sweet, but as soon as she would put me through to his crazy, it became cringe-worthy. I'm still a little afraid of him, so I'm not naming names. Plus, as I said before, I'm not paying for a lawyer.

Look, sometimes (like every day) people have to act fake in this industry. I suck at it, but when I had that manager, I knew I had to stomach the crazy for a season, until I could find someone better. It is better to have a bad rep than none at all. UNLESS you can't handle their crazy. In which case get away. It isn't worth the therapy.

If you decide to go with it for a second, for the sake of your future boyfriend/the world, please have someone or a few someones in your life who can bring some much-needed logic to the situation. Vent, laugh, step outside the crazy and remember who you are. I always say to myself, "*Not my circus, not my monkeys*" when I'm talking to crazy people. I realize that saying isn't my Oprah moment but it keeps the crazy in perspective.

You also have to set healthy boundaries. If hanging around and/or working with crazy is necessary for your career, don't get overly involved. The key to crazy is to love them from far away. Make them feel close, but keep your distance. Oh, and tap out before you pass out.

DREAM TEAM BREAKDOWN

Credit: Alphie Chikwashi

We all know you need your people, but *who* are they? Below is a breakdown of the people in our industry:

Photographers: These talented humans will help with content and capturing your personality and FLAWLESS beauty. For headshots, wear natural tank tops that bring out your eye color (no crazy patterns), full length shots in power stances (with a knee bent booty pop) to show your Queen-ness, and some fun ones that show your silly side. Your goal should be to work with press photographers or ones with a big social media following so you get distribution as well as great shots.

Stylists: Stylists help you slay the style game on the red carpet or in photoshoots. They will run around town pulling clothes, jewelry, and accessories to keep you looking and feeling FAB

Agents: Agents are the ones who pitch you for jobs and get you booked. They have relationships with casting agents and use a platform called "Breakdown Services" to see what acting roles are being cast.

Managers: Different from agents, managers focus on your brand and the direction of your career. They negotiate deals and review contracts but most will not actively pitch you.

Entertainment Attorneys: These power players will not only negotiate deals with their connections—they might help you land some.

Publicists: When you find the right one, you'll be in press constantly with strategic stories that tell the story you want to the media.

Coaches: Coaches can help with different sides of the industry. Whether you're figuring out your brand, learning how to give a fabulous audition or using improv to improve, these well-connected power players can help! Plus, they want to stay relevant to casting director and producer friends, so, if you have the talent, they might make a few intros. Aside from my speaking engagements, I coach aspiring entrepreneurs and talent on the Rachel McCord Show because just like these guys, I love to help.

Some people can't/won't help you in this town. Don't sweat it. Just keep playing the field until you find the perfect team who believes in you and knows what you need. Don't worry when you come across crazy people like my last manager. Just keep looking until you find the right ones. When you do, always show appreciation, kindness, love, and respect. Never take them for granted or become disloyal.

CONTACTING POTENTIAL AGENTS

Look, it isn't easy to land your team, but with the right talent and look, you can get there. Other than networking like we discussed in chapter ten, there are other ways to contact your potential team.

The first step is to find the addresses of the top agents, managers, and casting directors from lists from bookstores like Samuel French Film and Theatre. They share tips along with the mailing addresses for people you want to meet.

Credit: Hamid Moslehi

After you get their address, you need a fabulous cover letter that shares a short blurb of who you are. Include: 1) why you need representation, 2) something about you, and 3) how you can bring value. Remember to include all the appropriate sections that smart people teach you in school:

1. Salutation
2. Intro
3. Main point
4. The ask
5. The close

Don't say cheesy stuff like, "I'm your biggest fan." Being in entertainment, I'm sure they have crazier stalkers and psychos than you. If you're the craziest, I can't imagine that leading with that would be the smartest play. Just be honest and tell them you respect their work. Ask if you can buy them lunch.

The main point is covering how you can add value to their life. Maybe offer a blog post on each of their top clients. Use one line blurbs like, "*I have 200,000 fans on Instagram and just graduated from Juilliard.*" Umm, hi, Queen!

Just be sure to get to THE ASK. Don't shy away and send a confusing, long note. Keep it short, be respectful, ask directly, and give them an easy way to say yes - or easy exit if they can't do it. Hollywood is the land of slow nos. If you go on to be a huge star, they don't want to be the one who passed on <insert your name here>.

Just ask for fifteen minutes to hear about their success and get advice. Who doesn't love talking about themselves in the industry?

If you haven't yet moved to Hollywood, or wherever you dream of breaking into, try a legit networking campaign and visit a couple months before you move out. Contact all the people you would if you already lived there. When you get the meeting, and yes, I have faith that you will, conveniently forget to mention you don't live there. They won't rep you until you do.

Credit: Kelly McKeever

SLAY THAT MEETING

Before you go in, take the time to print your media kit, ready your sizzle and do your research, There's nothing worse than showing up without having your materials on fleek. Ask for advice from a trusted professional or friend in the industry. If they say something needs help, help it! Don't be lazy. Make it as fab as possible. You need to impress them.

Don't feel too cheesy to bring an orchid or bottle of a wine as a thank you. Energy and positivity will get you far in this industry. Don't play it too cool. Be fun, humble, excited, and grateful. Make sure you arrive fifteen minutes early, pick up the check and listen ... a lot.

Don't act aloof or entitled. Show that you're committed to your career and will do whatever it takes. If a reputable agency recommends you taking classes or getting new headshots, do it.

STAY ON THEIR RADAR

It's rare that agents offer contracts on the spot. It happened to me at Next Models, but I had been to many others and they didn't. Don't sweat it. Just be sure to send a thank you note right away. If you don't hear back or don't get the reply you were hoping for, follow up three to six months later. Maybe things have changed or maybe the person who said no isn't in power anymore. Casually stay connected every few months. Don't always talk business. Send them an invite to an event you heard about, wish them a happy birthday, etc. Stay connected and build a friendship.

TAKE REJECTION LIKE A PRO

Look, not everyone is going to see your fabness or be able to help you. It's annoying, we hate it, but it happens. Don't take it personally ... says everyone, every time. What the heck does that even mean? Basically, you need to make sure you remember how fabulous and beautiful you are. Successful people are insanely busy. I accidentally blow people off in this industry all the time because I straight up forget. It is never my intention to ghost them (unless they are crazy, in which case they might be on a blocked list of stalkers). But, for the most part it is just because life moves fast. I blink and four months, three shows, twenty photoshoots, and thousands of emails have gone by. It's not personal.

Remember it's a numbers game. We get rejected hundreds of times (that includes Katy Perry) before things click. Success isn't about never failing, it's about succeeding more than we do. Stay confident. All you need to do is build friendships. If you're talented, it might just come down to timing. Every time I get rejected, I work harder on my product (me, my deck, my resume, my humble brag, etc.). You won't win them all but you will win if you keep going. I've wanted to give up every week since I started. We're in this together. But I have accomplished more than I ever thought possible because I keep going.

DROP THE SOB STORY AND GET GLAM

Anytime you put yourself out there, whether you're at a casting or trying to win over a publicist, you'll get rejected. One of my favorite people, Andrea Feczko, a successful TV host, went out with me the other night and we started talking about *you.* That's right. My book is public at this point so I told her how much pressure I feel to make sure you find it helpful on your journey. She gave me some of the best advice about this industry. "*It is as much a mental game as it is a physical one.*" She is so right. This industry is about how you look, what you do, how talented you are, but the only ones who make it are the ones whose minds are up for the challenge. You'll have huge opportunities fall in your lap, but, if you are falling apart from the last rejection, you won't be able to hold it together long enough to werk it. No matter where you are at in your quest to SLAY THE FAME GAME (gosh, that sounded like some cheesy hero movie. My bad), you need to keep your mind clear and ready for success. Read empowering books, like: *The Slight Edge, 7 Habits of Highly Effective People, You can create an Extraordinary Life,* etc. Listen to podcast. Attend inspiring events. Commit to keeping your mind in the game and you'll SLAY!

Is there anything worse than a full-time mooch? You know these people. They can't keep or even land a job, and they end up blaming everyone and everything else but themselves. I'm hoping this isn't you. I know I make jokes about my man being my sugar daddy, but in reality, I have been supporting myself since I was thirteen. Working hard, saving, growing as a person and saying YES to the right things is how you monetize.

CHAPTER 14

MONETIZE, DUH: Brand Sponsorships

It wasn't always easy for me to deal with this side of the business. Negotiations, being comfortable accepting large sums of money (I didn't feel worthy of) and having big brands take risks on me was TERRIFYING. I realized that I was more afraid of success than I was failure, because I didn't feel comfortable being a person that others valued. By nature, creatives care more about their art than they do money. But, if we don't work against that, we will end up with a dream hobby instead of a dream career.

The only way to fix that is decide ... RIGHT NOW ... that you deserve success. That wealth works for you and that you're going to step into your power and OWN your place in the career world. Don't be afraid to be a sellout. See yourself as the BOSS Queen you are! Success and wealth are subjective. What you might consider success could be one dimensional for me or vice versa. Growing up with poor girl syndrome (which is basically believing "you don't deserve"), it took a hot minute to understand that success wasn't just about the money in my account. Success and wealth is a state of mind. It is an understanding that you're fabulous, you deserve, and, when opportunities you want come, you receive.

You won't start out getting paid in this industry. But once you've built a brand, gone on tons of castings, grown your fanbase, developed relationships and worked hard, it is freakin' time to start saying yes to revenue.

Whether you're in Hollywood, Atlanta, New York, or basically anywhere on social media, you'll realize that this is the only industry that will ask for so many freebies and opportunities in exchange for "exposure." That's the bad news. The good news is that this industry is full of FABULOUS opportunities ... paid or otherwise. Sometimes, you'll choose to judge that fashion show for free (like I'm doing tomorrow) because of the experience or the press. But the point is "you choose."

121

CHAMPAGNE TASTE, NO BUDGET

Before we can get you to the income generating BOSS Queen you are, we need to think about how you THINK about money. Are you a spender or a saver? Making money all day is great, but if you spend it all, you still won't have any. But don't worry, if there's one thing this girl (me) can do, it is stretch a dollar. I'm proud of my off-brand champagne sides. I don't mind being frugal and fabulous ... and neither should you.

Anyone can look fabulous in a custom tailored Dolce and Gabbana dress. It takes another kind of fabulous to make a clearance rack dress at Forever 21 look like you just walked off a Paris Fashion Week catwalk. I remember when I first moved to Hollywood, I thought my old fashioned tricks would work for me. Oh, hott-ness no! These people don't even chill on Runyon ... for a hike! People wear FULL makeup, coordinating outfits and jewelry ... the whole nine. Look, that's all great. You did read my tips to slay your style, right? But, it is a problem when people are so busy trying to fit in, they run out of money and end up on someone's couch. Not me (and not you); I know how to stretch my Benjamins.

Welcome to the life of the vagabond, where you don't know when your next check is coming. This is the land of feast or famine. One day, you might be stocking $10,000 and the next you might be stocking up on beans and rice. There isn't an accounting department sending your check every Friday at noon. You'll make money, then won't. If you live in Hollywood, you know what I mean. It is hard to live here and impossible to stay when you're broke.

Credit: Stephanie Girard

My girlfriend dated a guy who was really LA wealthy. You know, he had a G Wagon but no house, no furniture, no savings, etc. BUT he had that G Wagon. Look at my face ... eye roll on aisle three. What he OBVIOUSLY didn't get is that the key to off-brand champagne style is to leave your ego outside the shopping center. Sure, a G Wagon would be awesome, if you had a FREAKING garage to park it in! But, if you have no house ... you probably aren't ready for the dream car. You must learn how to live within your means. You never know when your next check will come. Sure, it might be a little embarrassing pulling up in Beverly Hills in a Honda Civic, but would you rather have a Honda and a home or a G Wagon and a truck stop shower? Eww.

Credit: Adam Kay

I'm going to help you learn to save money, live better. Just kidding, that's the Walmart slogan. But, I'll teach you the tips on looking "fabu*less*" i.e. saving cash while looking fab. I would much rather wear a $20 outfit, $80 bag and have $4,900 in the bank than have a $5,000 look that I can only wear once.

Before I learned my worth outside of material things, I remember landing my second job and splurging on my first Louis Vuitton. The White Multi Color Speedy 30 (just like Jessica Simpson). It was $2,400, but I was so excited because it was my "See, I'm not poor anymore!" message to the world. Of course, that was probably .00001% of Jessica's financial worth, while it was about 75% of mine. Material things feel (really) great for a hot minute until they, like every lonely item in the closet, lose their newness. They become old and boring like everything else.

You hold the power when you keep the moola. Sure, a 40% off sale is pretty dope, but not as dope as 100% off. Save your money. That way, if you have a dry spell with work, you won't also have a panic attack.

I'm always proud of myself when I opt for a night in with my Hulu when I could have gone to the movies and spent $30, or when I eat at home and just buy a drink when out with friends when I could have spent $75. The key is to make small sacrifices daily. Do you need the filet or would you be just as happy with the salmon? I know it sounds like a world of compromises but it's not. It is a world of small, smart decisions. Easy to do, just as easy not to do. If you game the system, you'll start to love it! If you spend $7 a day on coffee, it might not seem like much, but that is $2555, annually. It's the little adjustments that grow over time. Especially if you took that $2555, plus savings on those handbags and invested it into an index with compound interest. You could invest in your own Starbucks chain in a couple years. Talk about Queen-ness! I just want you to self-park, save, and still be fabulous!

Credit: Adam Kay

DO WHAT YOU LOVE

I don't like clichés. I don't like cheesy. And, I don't like corny. In fact, when people start saying cheesy things, I remind them how annoying their "corntricity" is. Yes, Google, I meant to say "corntricity." I'm a professional writer so that gives me carte blanche to make up words. Especially when the couple next to me is making out WHILE using baby talk. Look! He loves you more. Just get over it.

In this case, the cliché is right. They have all said it. No really, every single entrepreneur has told you, "Do what you love and you'll never work a day in your life." I thought it was a load of crap. It partially is. While building a brand is a LOT of work, it is incredibly rewarding.

When I started The McCord List, I developed a plan to bring in revenue to support my fun, fabulous lifestyle. I was promoting fashion and beauty brands in my press, social media, blog and on partner channels. The problem was, I HATED IT. I am talking: grumpy, angry, terrible-twos kinda annoyance. I thought, "If I can just become successful enough, I can hire someone to take this over and focus on what I love ... aka NOT this." That's because brands were treating me like an agency. When I stopped focusing my business model on the parts of the business I disliked, I got to lean into the parts I love! Now I'm licensing my name with brands I love. I'm involved in design, brand strategy, and marketing. I couldn't be happier! Sometimes the stuff you don't like leads you to the stuff you do! Tony Robbins (one of my favorite motivational speakers and authors) says that sometimes you just need a small shift in life to get where you want to be.

You can't experience that shift when you create negative energy and complain all the time. Successful people will move on quickly. I never hire people who talk about how bad life has been for them. I have been through a bunch of crap, but that is not what determines your mood or success. It is all based on what you choose to do with it. Are you going to let some crap bring you down or are you going to pull your crap up?

Just keep a positive attitude and have faith that whatever problems you're experiencing are preparing you for something. If I hadn't fallen on my face, gone broke, been pushed down by those I trusted, hated on by trolls or felt inadequate (pretty much every day), I wouldn't have the heart or understanding to help anyone. And, I know my life would be pretty empty if I didn't. I would be crazy to see emptiness and pain in this industry and the world and not do something. Especially since I have unique abilities to do so. Sure, there are parts of the business that I don't like. Ironically, most of them have everything to do with the fame game. If I had it my way, I would be sitting in sweats with my Chihuahuas writing books and having deep talks all day. I would be making the world a little more fabulous with a lot less pain. But there is an 80/20 rule in play. As long as you love 80% of what you do, you can push through that remaining 20%.

Find the things you LOVE and create a business model around it. When you do, make sure it is something the market needs. Then, you'll jump out of bed to do it each morning. You'll tell everyone about it because you passionately believe in it. That passion will get people passionate with you. When I made slight shifts to what I was doing, I started *loving* my work so much I would nerd out and tell everyone about it. I

MAKING THE SHIFT

Before I made that shift, I felt completely lost. I realized I was not living my passion but I had been trying to figure it out for so long, I was tired. I had built a ton of success and made The McCord List a public brand. Which was great but I had reached my wall. What was the point? I wasn't really helping anyone. That drove me crazy. I was just delivering amazing exposure for brands. I knew I couldn't do it much longer. I needed to make a change. I mean, I was getting stalked for reviews on mosquito repellants, people! Yes, someone sent me a mosquito repellant, and was hounding me for a review. I had that moment when I thought, *"What am I doing?"*

125

FROM
FREEBIES
MERCEDES

Credit Cameron Cone

Have you seen that HILARIOUS meme of a skeleton, passed out, with the words: *"Me waiting for that free work for "exposure" to pay off."* **LMAO.** CRYINGGG!!! People in entertainment feel this more than anyone. We love what we do so much we're willing to do it for free. Unfortunately, that kind of thinking doesn't translate into wealth.

<u>The type of thinking that translates into wealth is:</u>

- The willingness to work hard
- Strategy to build a brand with value
- Putting a number/rate on that value
- A willingness to overcome the uncomfortable feelings tied to asking for what you deserve

If you work hard and have amazing strategy (a mentor or plan), you can create anything. I started working when I was thirteen. I would clock out because my employer couldn't afford to pay me for the entire day. I cared more about my future than $10 hourly. I knew if I put the work in (brought value), I could learn everything there was to know about business. I did. Was I working at a talent agency, modeling or doing something I was passionate about? Nope. Sure, I was modeling on the side, but I was working at a pizzeria. Which I helped leverage into a full, Italian restaurant that I walked away from when offered my own location. I was eighteen. I had learned all I could/wanted to there. I wanted a career that required stilettos. I'm only halfway kidding. I knew I wanted to be a BOSS, I just didn't know where.

126

I got a job as one of the youngest employees at one of the largest corporations in the world and learned so much about business etiquette. It helped this homeschool girl without a college degree to sit across from CEOs and decision makers on the daily, talking business model and employee engagement strategy.

By the time I moved to Hollywood, I knew how to think like an entrepreneur. Keep costs down and revenues high. I learned that business comes down to two things: product and marketability. In the entertainment industry, you are the product. Your ability to brand and promote yourself is your marketability.

By now, I'm sure you see yourself as a brand. But, to monetize, you need to have or consider yourself to be a packaged product. How can you work with customers and clients? Social media for business is simply a revenue generator. The better your engagement and ability to move the masses, the higher your chances of product sales.

Let's break that down using The McCord List and me as the example:

1. I developed a brand around myself: The McCord List.
2. What was my product? Phase I, during the company build, was a community of influential women, myself included. We serviced clients (brands) by posting about their products on our respective channels (blogs, social media, podcasts, TV shows, etc.).
3. My public brand took off, we started focusing on having The McCord List and me promote the same clients (brands) with photoshoots, press, and my own respective channels.
4. I wrote SLAY THE FAME GAME.
5. We leveraged case studies from press activations using the "Rachel McCord Brand," which resulted in over 400 million media impressions, to start a new partnerships. We are now developing a product line that helps woman SLAY
6. We're now refocusing our attention (we had been too busy in the past) to grow my social media and move product (book, content series, and upcoming product line) to my NEW clients (end users, millennial women).

Does that make sense? When you take YOU out of the equation, and start seeing yourself as a PRODUCT or PRODUCT GENERATION tool, you can start to monetize on what you've built.

Whether you are selling to clients (brands/companies) or customers (end users), you can use social media to attract your target. You just need to be smart. If you want brands to pay you to advertise, you need to have a marketing strategy for how to reach them. If social media is your only marketing tool, you had better make sure your content is speaking directly to your target client/customer.

YOU DESERVE IT, QUEEN!

To take yourself out of the awkward feeling that you're selling yourself, you might need to do a little self work. As my amazing therapist always reminds me, it doesn't need to feel totally comfortable ... you just need to do it. We are going deep!

This should be your favorite chapter. I mean, we know they *all* are! Okay, technically *we* don't know (and by "we" I mean "me"), 'cause I don't know ... which is exactly why I'm starting to feel a little insecure right about now ... Eek. You know what? Let's just move on ... This chapter is about trading that overdraft protection for some extra zeros in your account.

We all know there's a (long) season in the industry of volunteering and doing freebies. You need to do it to get your name out there, network, learn and grow. But, if you ever want to park that Prius, and start rolling in your wealth, you need to know when it's time to start charging your worth.

> I remember my first paycheck in Hollywood. It was $100 for a film cameo. I know that is SO tiny, but I was so proud to have made my first dollar in the industry, that I sent a screenshot to all my close friends back at home in Georgia ... cropping out the amount (obviously). *Surprise, Kathy D.! It wasn't that impressive! Oops!*

Especially when you think of how hard I worked hard for that check. In fact, that $100 probably cost me about $7,500, if you sum up all the rent, gas, parking meters, lunches, makeup, hair, celebratory lunches (after surviving each casting I didn't book), etc. That was the most expensive $100 I've ever made. But, don't worry, it was worth all the early call times, parking tickets, DIY makeup, Red Bulls, and co-star attitudes (are they really called my costars, if I wasn't even a star? Hmmmm...), etc. Whatever! Hair flip on fleek because I had ARRIVED. I was finally legit ... sort of.

Of course, that is not the type of monetization we're talking about in this chapter. But, it does tell the story of how hard we work. Those little expenses add up. So, make sure you're generating revenue however you can.

Remember, people will gladly *not* pay you. They don't become wealthy in this industry by throwing money around or leaving it on the table. You don't want to do that either. I had this brand reach out, eager to work with me. They didn't want to pay anything so we went back and forth. Finally, we agreed on a number and I started modeling for their campaigns. Then, I realized the money didn't make sense for how much I was (not) being paid. Once I told them I was walking, they said they can pay me whatever it takes. Are you kidding me? All this time they had a bigger budget? Sometimes brands want to test your abilities before they pay anything. If you're confident in your results you can do this, as long as you keep your boundaries in check and don't do it forever.

Don't worry, we aren't the only ones who struggle with asking for our worth. Entrepreneurs everywhere feel this. In fact, the owner of a jewelry store was having a hard time putting a price on her pieces, while her $20 an hour employee didn't think twice about it.

The most annoying question of last year was, "How much do you charge for an Instagram post?" Ahhh, I couldn't stand it! I would feel weird and think, "*Well, we're friends so maybe I shouldn't charge ...*" It was so awkward. If someone asked you right now what would you say? The biggest mistake we often make in this scenario is responding with, "*What's your budget? What would you pay?*" Of course, it is our way of deflecting so we stay comfortable. But, it sends the message that we don't see our own value. If we don't, why should they? When I made the decision to stop doing free work, it was like people just knew. There wasn't a big conversation, I just started weeding out the scrappers who weren't serious.

Does your value increase or decrease with each brand's budget? Of course not. We're just as fabulous in front of one brand as we are with the other. So, know your rate and stick with it.

You're beautiful. You have worth. You're more powerful, fabulous, and amazing than you know. It's time you start putting that value where it belongs. Besides, in this industry, the more you cost, the more people want you.

Credit: Stephanie Girard

YOU'VE GOTTA START SOMEWHERE

What have you accomplished so far with your career? Have you already been working as talent or are you just getting into it? Whether you come from an office job or a long list of successful photo shoots and films, everything you have done has prepared you for this. Believe that and create a portfolio that shows evidence of it. Working hard in other industries and building success and savings gave me invaluable confidence. Confidence I needed when I decided to figure out the entertainment industry from the inside out eight years ago. Eek, that sounds so long ago.

Whether you're working as a waitress (how I started my career) or assisting (how I started in Hollywood), you're learning business, so give it your all. You never know where it will lead. Everything I've done has taught me something. Good or bad. I worked as my sister's assistant in Hollywood when I first moved out here. Was it my favorite job? What do you think? Did I learn a ton, meet a bunch of people and develop as a business? Absolutely! Had I not accepted that opportunity, I wouldn't be in this city, let alone this industry. Now, I'm writing a book about it! I never would have guessed this would be my life. But I wouldn't change it for the world ... except maybe a ranch in Georgia riding horses on the daily.

WORKING WITH BRAND SPONSORS

Be flexible and think outside the box when working on your business model. Hollywood has experienced some massive shifts in content creation. Some studio executives are trying to ride out the "storm" while others are leaving and pursuing other areas of the industry. People have even called it the "Wild, Wild West.".

Industry changes are great news for content creators with a fanbase. If you own the audience, you have the power. It used to be only the studios with connection to fans. They decided what got made and what didn't. Now, any person with an iPhone or Canon can create content and get people to watch it.

By now, if you create content, you should know your strategy. But, how do you get paid for it? If you want an empire and tons of revenue, you have to think long-term. The goal is to build up your brand until you can be the face of a big brand. My man taught me early on with The McCord List that licensing my name for a product line or collection was the smartest route. I was in!

But, let's say you created your own show, built up an audience, and are now ready for sponsors. Awesome. Before you can pitch a brand, you need to know what they care about. It's all about sales. More than exposure, they want conversions (potential customers who actually buy). Some talent stops at the promise of exposure. Exposure is great and since they can't actually promise sales, I get it. But you want the brand to know you're in it with them. You want your audience to buy so the brand keeps advertising. That being said, you also need to keep your fans happy. They don't want some cheesy ad. If you want a win / win (which you do), you need fun content that fits the style your people are used to, with a product that fits their lifestyle. I wouldn't sell camping gear, but I would sell a clothing line.

Credit: Hamid Moslehi

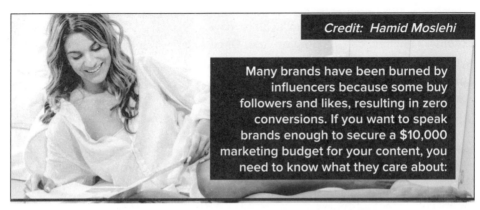

Many brands have been burned by influencers because some buy followers and likes, resulting in zero conversions. If you want to speak brands enough to secure a $10,000 marketing budget for your content, you need to know what they care about:

1. Real eyeballs
2. Your fanbase demographic/ psychographics (the age, income, passions of the people you reach)
3. Positive content
4. Lift in sales
5. Rights for use in marketing

The way to communicate the above is through a deck. A deck is basically a presentation that takes the reader through the story of you as a brand. You want your deck to give reasons why a brand, company, or potential partner would want to work with you. They need to see your vision and the design needs to be BEAUTIFUL. If they are going to go into business with you, they need to see alignment in design, content, and targeted demographic. Take your time on this. I recommend hiring an agency to create this for you. My man's company, LaunchPreneur, helps brands connect with the right people. So, reach out if you need a referral.

Below are a few tips that I've learned from working with every brand from JustFab and TopShop to McDonald's and Samsung. The number one tip is to not be afraid. Be willing to pitch brands from their website, social media, or after you meet them:

- Follow up and send a deck ASAP (within 24 hours).

- Follow up is EVERYTHING. Don't be afraid to casually ping them every few weeks.

- Get agreements in writing. I highly recommend using a lawyer for this. Liability sucks!

- Do what you promise, promptly and with professionalism.

- Send a follow up report with analytics and links to content.

- Ask for their business again.

- Always use spell check.

- Use a professional email address. Sorry Gmail!

- Get to the point quickly and strategically. Five sentence emails are perfect.

- Get on a call as quickly as possible.

- Don't "water hose" them with every idea that comes in your head. Keep it conversational.

- Build a rapport quickly. Ask what they are focused on, pitch your idea highlighting the ways you'll help them achieve their current goals.

- Ask them how you did and if they recommend any improvements.

Remember, it costs a LOT to acquire new clients. Lunches, calls, follow up, etc. Once you have them, keep them happy. That way they will use you over and over. Brands prefer to work with people and products they know and love.

NEGOTIATE LIKE A BOSS

Credit: Britt Barrett

If pitching yourself is too uncomfortable, consider having someone else pitch and negotiate for you. Or, maybe use that assistant email alias to give you some extra courage. If you decide to bring on a partner, make sure that person possesses skills you don't and is ready to work hard with you. Then respect their unique skills and don't try to make them like you. Pitching and negotiation takes a lot of follow up. When a deal is on the table, there's a lot of momentum. You don't want to let it die down.

If you negotiate your own deals, here's a few things you need to get comfy with ... quick.

1. Being uncomfortable
2. Walking away from a bad deal
3. Being okay in silence ... the awkward kin
4. Asking for and requiring what you're worth
5. Reminding them what you bring to the table

I found myself in my first intense negotiation over a brand deal. I had a meeting their office and was expecting my man to meet me there. I just wanted to sit the like talent who "had absolutely no idea what he was talking about." Ha! (course, I had actually told him exactly what I wanted. I started to panic a littl when he said he couldn't make it. "*Umm, what!!*" I thought. How was I going handle this one? The same way I have done everything else in my life ... Nike Ju Do It style. I took a deep breath and walked inside ...

I knew the intense negotiation was coming but I wanted to build a rapport/delay the inevitable with nervous talking. I was hiding it well but I was freaking out on the inside. They had no idea I was taking deep breaths and reminding myself over and over: "*You can always walk away. Be comfortable in the uncomfortable. Get ready for the AWKWARDDDDD silence.*"

We sat down and got into the intense stuff. I broke my own rule by asking what they wanted to offer, but they weren't going down that easy. Especially the woman in the corner who was more intense that a shark bite. They were like, "*No, you need to make us an offer.*" Eww. Who even says that? I thought, "*Whatever, let's do this,*" then took a deep breath, blacked out a little and told them what I wanted. They started trying to negotiate, but I had come in with the offer I wanted to walk out with. This isn't a used car dealership. This is my name, brand and likeness. I'm not about to haggle. I figured, if they don't understand what I bring to the table, I'm not going into business with them. Well, it WORKED! I got the offer and contract within a week. It was nerve-wracking but I learned three surprising and invaluable lessons that day ...

1.   I actually like negotiation and feel empowered asking for what I want
2.   I'm pretty freaking good at it ... if I do say so myself
3.   I'm stronger than I realized ...

... and so are YOU!

133

Credit: Britt Barrett

Don't just rely on brand sponsors to monetize, there are plenty of ways to bring value and extract cash from it. The way to do that is to first know who has the money and what they want.

Studios and networks are the people who cut the checks for film and TV projects. They greenlight what happens and pass on what doesn't. If you have your own YouTube channel, you get to call the shots and the greenlight. But you have to figure out how you're going to get revenue.

YouTube allows you to turn on AdSense, but that's peanuts. Big endorsement deals are where you make the real G's—which basically means the cash ($1,500-$5,000++, depending on your fan base). You like my gangsta side? No? Okay. Moving right along.

There are many ways for you to monetize while doing what you love ... here's a list to get you started:

- Get approved for Like.To.Know.It, and monetize with a commission on every outfit you post. This is one of those affiliate programs that is great when you're starting out. Just don't be hurt if you aren't approved at first. I wasn't and most of my friends weren't either. Just keep growing and building your brand and check back later.
- Study an area of the industry and become a coach at it. You could charge anywhere from $50-$500 an hour, depending on how fabulous you are and how high the demand.
- If you decide to coach, make sure your blog content is amazing! That's the best way to promote your mad skills and to prove that what you teach can actually help your potential clients.
- Become a freelance blogger.

- Create an online course with Udemy, Teachable, or Course Merchant. You can also use a premium online course plugin directly from your blog, if you use Word Press. They have Zippy Courses, CoursePress, WP CourseWare and Woothemes Sensei

- Write a book (what a genius idea!) =)

- Book speaking engagements

- Make specialty jewelry

- Produce content for brands: fashion meet JustFab, makeup tutorials meet NARS, pranks meet whoever fits that demographic, I know nothing about it. #oops

- License your name for a collection (once you have SLAYED the fame game)

- Work in-house for a company as a blogger, photographer, or model

I just named a bunch, but why not start thinking of other things you can do to monetize? It will be a fun exercise and who knows, maybe you end up with the next BOSS idea! I believe in you, Queen!

CHAPTER 15

Stay smart in this industry. Making one bad choice can easily lead to so many others. Stay away from crazies, the casting couch, and anything that makes you uncomfortable. To help you navigate, I wrote this chapter to share a bunch of random advice to keep you from making costly mistakes that my friends and I SLAYED! What? We didn't have this book.

For me, one of my bigger mistakes was who I dated. Who you hang with really matters, but who you date can *really* mess you up! Dating in Hollywood isn't easy. Especially for a romantic, naive, Southern girl with a LOT to learn. I can't even tell you how crazy my first relationship out here was. That's the second book!

#1 DO YOU, QUEEN!

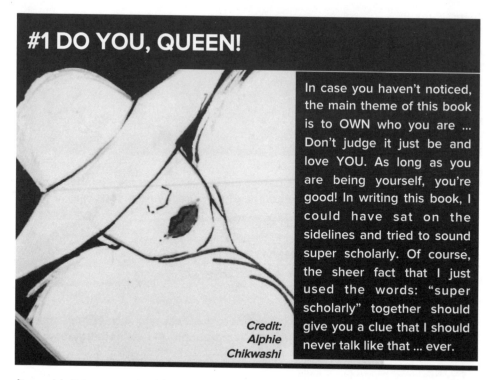

Credit: Alphie Chikwashi

In case you haven't noticed, the main theme of this book is to OWN who you are ... Don't judge it just be and love YOU. As long as you are being yourself, you're good! In writing this book, I could have sat on the sidelines and tried to sound super scholarly. Of course, the sheer fact that I just used the words: "super scholarly" together should give you a clue that I should never talk like that ... ever.

It wouldn't have worked because I would have been so busy trying to sound smart, I would've bored us both to tears. Instead, when I decided to own my ME, this book flowed insanely fast as a result. In fact, I wrote close to 30,000 words in two and a half weeks. And, the most important part, is I have been having a blast! When you're being your full, uninhibited self, you'll move faster than you ever would have imagined.

Credit: Cameron Cone

> Just remember, whatever "owning all colors of you" looks like, you've got to do it. If it doesn't fit your brand, maybe you need to revisit chapter three and change it up a little. Focus on that passion and the rest will work itself out.

Being yourself 100% while creating content is a little scary at first, and it's uncomfortable knowing people can see the number of likes and views you get (or don't get). But, as long as you're being yourself and having fun with it, you won't really care. Trust me! =)

#2 NEVER, EVER COMPROMISE WHO YOU ARE

This industry will ask a lot of you. They might even try and make you feel bad when you say no to something ... DON'T! I still regret this tiny cameo I made in a film where I used some nasty language the non-acting me would NEVER do.

Never show more, say more, do more, or go along with more than you feel comfortable with. If people don't get it, show them the door. You're a fabulous Queen! Your success is not determined by how famous, wealthy or in demand you are, your success should always be based on how you feel in your heart. We all have different versions of what it means to SLAY THE FAME GAME. Never look back with guilt when you say no. Respect it—I do.

#3 IGNORE THE 💩 IN THE BUSINESS

Please, do us all a favor (me, you, your future self), STAY AWAY FROM THE CRAZIES. This industry has its fair share. So, STAY AWAY! You need to focus on how you feel when you spend time with people you meet. Fortunately, that shouldn't be too hard because if there's one thing you can get away with (and will actually fit in on) in Hollywood, it's focusing on you. *wink* Make sure the people, places, and things you surround yourself with leave you feeling positive and inspired. If not, show yourself the door.

When success hits, people will appear out of EVERYWHERE with every offer, excuse and reason under the sun to work with you. The fame game has its perks. But you have to know when to take a breather. I don't like being stalked. I'm not talking about the paps (I actually call them—what? They are my friends). I'm referring to psycho texts, emails, phone calls, etc.

As a Scorpio, sometimes, I just want to disappear. Not forever (I love my life). Just long enough to clear my brain out. That's hard to do when people breathe down your neck ... Love you, but need to get away from you.

> Me: *"Oh, now that you've called five times, left six voicemails* (do the math on that one), *texted me nineteen times, and sent a pigeon with a love letter, I have finally decided I want to hang out."* I'm kidding ... ish.

Nah, I really am joking! I love everyone but sometimes I just need to take a Rachel minute, and be alone. I'm basically the puppy mommy version of a cat lady. You might be thinking, "What on EARTH does this have to do with me avoiding the 💩 in the business??" Well, I have prepared a trusty AVOID list to help you do just that:

BEACH BALL CRAZY

Have you ever seen someone try to sit on a beach ball underwater? They might be able to keep that crazy down for a solid thirty seconds but it doesn't take long before that crap shoots straight up out of the water, knocking over anyone in its way. If you've ever seen a reality show, you've seen this happen. Only, instead of a beach ball, we're talking about a crazy human on the wrong side of nuts.

This is the perfect (worst) character of a reality show. Their *"Somebody better hold me back right now"* level of crazy always makes them infamous ... and, unemployed. Sponsoring brands won't touch them, people won't hire them, and smart people won't hang with them ... including you and me.

NARCISSISTS

Ugh. These are the people who can't hear you talk over the arrogance in their head. They are so busy making the world about them, they successfully tune everyone else out. You are basically their audience and *"All the world's a stage."*

They are so obsessed with being perfect, they become perfectly calculated weirdos. Success comes with catlike strategy. The thought goes like this, *"I am going to hug you in 3, 2, 1, next, I will raise this flute of champagne and laugh in 3, 2, 1. Then, I will humbly tell you about my recent shoot* (from three years ago) *and brag about my role as spokesmodel for the world."* And all that happens when you ask them where the bathroom is.

USERS

Oh, my personal non-favorite. What would we do without the users in the industry? The ones who don't care if you are struggling, stressed, overworked, or ready to give up. As long as you spend your last $7 on their latte, they are good! The rationale is pretty impressive, even for them. They will give you a million reasons why they ask for everything you own, and then a million excuses as to why they can't give ANYTHING to you. The struggle is real and so is the headache they bring on. They are like narcissists... on crack.

If you encounter these ... umm, unwanted miagraines, find some Tylenol and hair flip your way out of there!

Credit: Leo Deveney

CHAPTER 16
GIRL BYE: MIC DROP

I can't believe this crazy journey has come to a close. Now that I'm about to say goodbye, my sensitive side is kicking in like a nerd. I'm so thrilled —ahh that's such a corny way to say how I feel! I'm so freaking happy you came on this crazy ride with me. I realize I'm a whole lotta' whole lotta ... thanks for hanging in there (or skipping to the end). The good news is, you're going to do great ... thanks to me! Haha! JK. Thanks to YOU! You are a freaking star. I already know it. I am so excited for you. I am excited for what's to come in your life. I can't wait to see you in Hollywood or on social media SLAYING the GAME!

Credit: Britt Barrett

Always remember, you have more power than you know. Don't ever underestimate your abilities. Fame isn't the end all, I hope you've learned that from this book. It is just a tool to use on the journey (gosh, my cheesy is so loud right now!) of your fabulous life. Whether you see social media or Hollywood as the place for you or I have scared you off (I didn't say fame was for everyone). The one thing I really want to leave you with is the one thing all this crazy Hollywood crap has taught me ... no matter where you grew up, what kind of education you have (or don't have), how you look, or how much (or little) you have, you can achieve anything you dream of. The truth is, *SLAY THE FAME GAME* isn't about "fame" at all. It's about going for it with everything you've got! Never count yourself out and never sell yourself short. No matter what you want, what you dream, what you find important. Believe in yourself and know that you were born to SLAY.

I love you always, Rach xo

ACKNOWLEDGEMENTS

Are you ready

for my acknowledgments? You know, the part of the book that really annoys readers, but reminds the author of just how popular they are? Well, get ready because I'm VERY popular. Besides, we all know I'm NEVER getting that OSCAR ...

First, foremost, and always, I want to thank **God**. It's His breath in my lungs ... so He's the one allowing me to annoy the world with my weirdness. I'm joking! In all honestly, I know I would never be here if it weren't for HIM. He has loved me, helped me, and held me when I needed Him most ... Thank you for giving me life to the fullest!

I'm so, so grateful for my person. My best friend. My champion. The first person to make it his mission in life to LAUNCH me (he is to blame, you guys). Thank you, my Ricky, for being my fire, inspiration, love, hubby, and every beat of my heart. You make me who I am. You hold me up when I am afraid. You challenge me to live my potential and you catch me every time I fail ... like, badly. I love you so much, my sugar daddy!

To my little furry babies, Giggles and Munchkin. (Don't worry) I'm wise enough to know you'll NEVER read this but I wouldn't be me if I didn't mention you, my little munchkins! Thank you for loving me during my unlovable moments, and cuddling with me in the floor of the closet when the world is just too scary and big. You've been there through so many laughs, cries, joys, and sorrows in the past ten years. Thank you for fooling me into thinking I was the one saving y'all! I love you, my little babies!

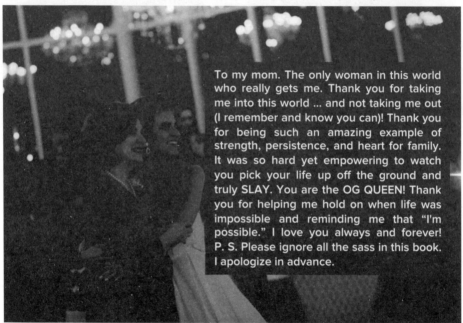

To my mom. The only woman in this world who really gets me. Thank you for taking me into this world ... and not taking me out (I remember and know you can)! Thank you for being such an amazing example of strength, persistence, and heart for family. It was so hard yet empowering to watch you pick your life up off the ground and truly SLAY. You are the OG QUEEN! Thank you for helping me hold on when life was impossible and reminding me that "I'm possible." I love you always and forever! P. S. Please ignore all the sass in this book. I apologize in advance.

To my sisters: Angel, thank you for being such a beautiful heart, full of adaptability, forgiveness, and love! You are my big sissy, and I love you! AnnaLynne, thank you for everything you do to make the world a better place. I'm so proud of you! Thank you for being such an example to remind me to believe in myself and GO FOR IT in life. I love you!

To my Daddy: I am so grateful to have you in my life. You are always the one I want to take notice! I love you so much! Thank you for all the Little Debbie's and Dollar Tree trips. Amy: You are such a gem! You are beautiful, fun, and kind! Thank you for all the love! xoxo

 For my little man (aka brother), Jonathan: With your limited, three-year-old vocabulary, I know we haven't had many deep discussions, but you need to know how much you light up my life! I love you very much, and am always here for you. P.S. I'm little pissed that you knocked me out as the baby in the family, but with those eyes and that hair ... you are forgiven!

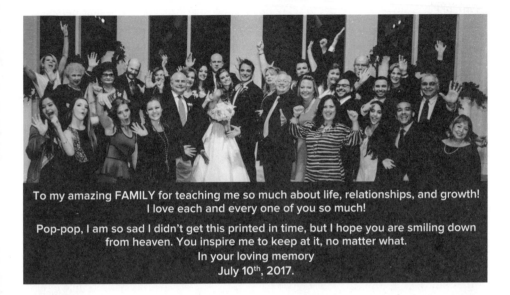

To my amazing FAMILY for teaching me so much about life, relationships, and growth!
I love each and every one of you so much!

Pop-pop, I am so sad I didn't get this printed in time, but I hope you are smiling down
from heaven. You inspire me to keep at it, no matter what.
In your loving memory
July 10th, 2017.

To Scott and Theresa Beck, I truly wouldn't be here today if it weren't for your love, support, and help in my healing. Thank you for believing in who I could be. I have more respect, love, and admiration for you both than you will ever know. I'm forever humbled by your love. Thank you for being the OG champions!

To Kathy, thank you for believing I was a superstar when all I had accomplished in life was knocking out Newman... our robotic mailman. You represent such class and beauty. Thank you for inspiring me to push past who I was to become who I am. I credit you for all the good sides of me ... and hope you can continue to laugh at the other parts! Here's to Irish Pubs, short men, and fabulous glasses of Chardonnay and bubbly!

Blaire, you are my spirit animal. You were the most gorgeous partner-in-crime for all those club sneaks in and are now the most beautiful best friend a girl could ask for.

To: Sherry, Heather, Heidi, Jess, Ryan, Kellan, Kim, TJ, Britt, Alexia, Caitlin, Colin, Brave, Virginia, Johnny, Henry, Angela, Kristen, Kris, Aurora, Jimmy, Elizabeth, Caroline, Megan, Joey, Hilary, Tracy, Russ, Danny, Josh, thank you all so much for loving me and welcoming me into your EPIC family. I'm so lucky to call you my people in this insane town of Hollywood!

Katie, we always knew the craziest ones were the funniest. Thank you for being freaking hilarious with me. Hollywood is dull without you!

Hanna Hunt, thank you for all the encouragement, laughter, painting sessions, Netflix and chill time and all the crazy, post-TK. I love you, boo!

143

Krista, you have been such a light in my light, over the last few months. I know we are new BFFs, but it didn't take long for me to FALL IN LOVE! You are amazing, inside and out. I love you and am so grateful for you!

Harmonie, you are such a remarkable woman! The way you SLAY THE GAME with everything you touch is absolutely inspiring. Thank you for believing in me and for sharing your amazing encouragement while I was writing this book.

Thank you, Christine, Oliver, Doug, Olga, Mini Me Emily, for being my Hollywood people. I love you all so much! Christine, thank you for believing in me when I didn't believe in myself (way before that Vogue feature that made me cry ... and cry ... and cry).

Nick Movs for being my favorite (fabulous) song! You inspire me to think BIG and stay hot... like a Bentley.

Dr. Kupper, you truly are the best therapist in Hollywood. I don't know how (or why) you put up with me. But thank you for teaching me how to cope, learn, love, and grow. I know for a fact that I wouldn't have made it without you! Thank you for not kicking me out ... yet!

To Esther, Whitney, and the GORGEOUS ladies of The Fedd Agency. I can't believe you believe in me. I am BEYOND grateful and humbled by you. I love y'all more than you'll ever know! Let's keep hair flippin' through many more books in the future.

Thank you to every fabulous blogger, influencer, celebrity, and Hollywood sister who I know and love. You have inspired this book and helped me own my fabulous. Let's go on and remind those #haters how much work it really is to be us. Never give up. Keep posing, snapping, and laughing (on cue) for that perfectly posed candid.

Thank you so much to everyone else who has inspired, loved, laughed with (and at) me. You know who you are (but this is my first book and I'm scared people will stop reading if I go on much longer). But, I love you. Mean it. You know it.

Now, I'm going to thank myself. Haha! I'm just kidding. But me, myself and I are all very excited that we can finally cash in on all those unpaid selfies.

 DROP.